VERSES *from a* TWISTED MIND

JORDAN A RIPPEL

Tellwell Talent
www.tellwell.ca

ISBN
978-0-2288-1223-4 (Hardcover)
978-0-2288-1222-7 (Paperback)
978-0-2288-1224-1 (eBook)

Acknowledgement

First off, I would like to acknowledge a person very special to me. My true best friend, my twin. In the process of editing and picking from ungodly amounts of poems I have written, my sister Nicole R Frech has been a huge support and driving force in not only life in general, but this book which has been a dream of mine for years. Just as I, she is also poetically gifted and has written some extraordinary pieces. She has a vocabulary I wish I could achieve, as well as that true female perspective that is the other side of a coin in which I only wish we could all catch a glimpse of. Nicole is not just my friend, my twin, my support but also my sledding and adventure buddy. In fact, one adventure we had together last winter inspired a creation in which we both contributed to and she put together and I would like to share it with you. Enjoy!

Hiding Creek

In oilfield country
Close to the border between Alberta and BC
There lies a narrow, winding road
Meant for rigs hauling a load

A shortcut taken
On our way home from mountain adventure
Darkness descended as twilight turned to night
Still buzzing on adrenaline
From trees dodged, hills scaled

Taking corners at speeds too fast
Trees a blur as we fly past
Drifting with a trailer like a boss
Running on hope the sleds don't' get tossed

Headlights appear suddenly, two vehicles we met
Almost didn't stand a chance
Pretty sure they shit their pants
Sideways, taking both lanes, on hand on the wheel
Casual tip of the hat as we Tokyo drift pass

Brakes applied, panicked cries
Nowhere to go, snowbanks high on either side
A collision avoided by a hair
The fate of that night seems fair

I told you to keep in the down low
What happened on the Hiding Creek Road
Stays there, Bro

Just a Thought

Kept in corners, tortured and soulless is this what is meant to be?

Scattered shards of glass surround you, reflecting on all the tortures from the past, leaching the demons out from hiding.

As cold as the concrete beneath hearts brittle and not complete, for life has proven to be a battle we can't defeat so why carry on this way?

Is it addiction to being beaten down and drug violently through coarse ground?

Or is it just the glimpses of triumph that keep us trying?

Trying to refrain from crying out for help in forms of a violent yelp like a dog with a broken spine.

Keep dragging this on like there's some sort of end, light at the other side, or until we give up and die, for this is all but an unwritten plan.

Don't walk in my shoes, a lonely heart that's been fucking abused, for I am nothing more than man.

My lines at best need autocorrect because I'm losing my ways.

No sorrow for me please, you haven't even seen the evil lurking within, I keep it hidden from the people for no one needs this evil, so I let it shred me inside.

No where to turn, no where to hide, letting this blood and pain fill inside till my eyes can't open again.

I am just a man.

On Trial, Under Oath

So, each day is gift and this life is what we make it.
They say that the sun is shining, and depression is non-existent.
I got pulled aside and asked a personal question.
They say life is better than what you are depicting.
So why is it that you always lean to the black when you are writing?

You need to get some help, man, you need to seek some counseling.
Your words are giving me a fairly certain impression.
That you clutch this darkness, you crave depression.
I read a lot of your work and its just dark minded based perceptions.
Where's the light, man? Where's the happy endings?
Why can't you see the beauty on the ground you're walking?
The sun that's right above you.
The songs the birds sing, man, open your mind to something beautiful.

I kinda sat back and re-thought my answer.
You know, cause there is three sides to that coin within perspective.
I reached inside my minds collection.
Remembering little quotes and passages I have written.
Then like that, it hits me.
Like the volume on the sun turned up past blinding.
Like every hue of color, vivid and visually exploding.

Yeah, I tend to pen in darkness; I sit in my basement of collections.
Memories, moments and stored emotions.
I write it out as I empty bottles.
Release the pent-up anger and all forms of absorbed emotions.
See, I think if it's my words that strike you, bend your mind and lower vibrations.
Then it's not really my demons that need exorcising, because I just triggered something within your own dungeon.

Put my lyrics under analytical lenses.
Pull them apart and dissect the meanings.
Your gonna find a lot of truth within ribbons of depression.
I just write about the real things, the stuff we are all scared of.
Call me a counselor, only I have lived through it.
I have seen, heard, and helped them face it.
How many people have you made feel?
How many times have you been told your words have helped people?
Yes, what I write tends to be lower; yes, what I say is heavy on the shoulders.

But if I don't shed light on the mind that runs depressive.
Then the ones closest wouldn't have an understanding.
See, I lived it and I still come out swinging.
I pen this out using not just my own emotions.
Turns out I'm a great listener, cause the stories I have heard have helped formed opinions.
I write about life as I have seen it.

Seriously though, the sun's out and everyone sees it.
The grass is green in the fields.
The flowers are vivid, and the birds are singing.
Blue sky, cloud figures and rainbows.
Just go outside or look through a window.
It's a given and it is always available.
Happy go lucky, love and laughter.
Over and over and over.
So, forgive me if I bring light on the shadows.

Forgive me for penning about the struggles.
Yeah, forgive me for telling stories.
I'm just not afraid of those deranged demons.
So, if it makes you feel something different
Form opinions laced in darkness, then clearly you focus on the evil.
Cause I have a lot of hope and fighting spirit within my scriptures.
So maybe you have a darkness that you have been supressing.
Maybe you should take your own advice and seek some counseling.
Miss me with that self-help stuff cause I'm a fighter.
Still living, riding, writing, laughing and breathing.

I'm in my lane, why are you swerving?
Put me under a spotlight and dissect me.
Pin me as dark, low and suicidal.
Paint me black like Wednesday Adams paints a rainbow.
Plaster me with labels or just avoid me.
Think what you want, it won't make a difference.
The ones who have gotten to know me, know that I'm actually a great person and they think I'm
funny.
My day ones are the only ones whose opinions kinda matter.

But if you haven't noticed, the suns out and the ravens are singing.
Listen closely, you will here the sirens.
The medics, the first responders.
Glass breaking and lives being shattered.
Let's get out there and just enjoy it!
We all have a different experience.
Your great day could be someone's rock bottom.
Stay in your lane and don't take things too literal.
Stories are stories, knowledge at your disposal.
Don't read what I write and think you know me.
If you would like to, then get a hold of me.
Seriously, I'm waiting.

Epitaph

An epitaph wrote on the walls inside, not a single breath or day goes by.
Pinnacle scars in the life once endured.
Now nothing is left, yet the memories live.

Lights that burn.
The lights that blind.
It's the lights that tend to cauterize our eyes.
Candles lit at both ends.
Living so fast, always leaving too soon.

An epitaph scribed on the walls deep inside.
Lyrics of you and what you brought to my life.
Replaying photos, stories in my mind.
The good times and the ones that absorb some of the light.

All of the time that I wish I didn't waste.
All of the tears I never thought I would taste.
That contagious smile that would infect my face.
The words in silence when you were so close.

An epitaph of you scribed in my soul.
If you only knew, if I could have shown.
Sometimes the truth tears at the throat.
Words that never come, then you watch them go.

One more day, oh just one more.
Beg and plead as you barter with ghosts.
Feel that presence when you know they're close.
The shivers that go right to your toes.

I was given a message from the greatest unknown.
They hear your pleas and they can be so close.
Sit with you even when you boarded up your doors.
Sometimes they try and hug the hurt in your soul.

They try to rearrange and connect to your source.
The love that they give is beyond immeasurable.
Listen to the voice, subtle but pure.
They are offering advice, a guidance to better light.

Though times get tough and emotions die.
Not everything destroyed has to lay in a grave out of sight.
Loss of that trait, the humility and love.
That's the beginning to the end of life.
For if you aren't dead, there is no reason to not have some light.

Sitting idle and wasting time.
Reading the epitaph for you in my mind.
The wisdom, the smiles, the laugh and the life.
The things I need most in this moment in time.
For not a second goes by, not a single day, you don't cross this twisted mind.

The Call to Break the Bind

Can't help but think back to being ten.
Convinced I'd never make it far.
Life's a race that nobody wins.
Thoughts and plans that blacken the purest soul.
Embraced the goat's presence as the evil takes control.

Never thought I would see a day.
Never wanted to get this far.
Plagued the entire way, been drowning in my hole.
So, Satan, can you hear me now? Feel me losing control?
Dark wraith hovers overhead, take me out if you think you have a chance!

Background noise, words that echo to the core.
Take that darkness back, as I wear it like a new wardrobe.
Fuck you if you think I'll be safe behind closed doors.
Judge me all you want but you cunts don't even know.
Satan hear me now; I challenge you for your throne!

Since the age of ten, waiting for the day I lose hope.
Well that day has come, thanks for showing me the door.
Blood soaked pentagram I drew upon the floor.
Summon the demon screaming, I'm gonna lose control.
I bottled so much anger and now it's gonna flood my world.
Motes won't save a soul; nothing will contain what I have yet to show.

I will sacrifice the next fucking soul.
I swear to Satan and his army I'm here to tear some throats.
Test me not unto despair cause I have vanquished my self control.
Tempt me not in person cause I have nothing left to lose.
Fuck with me in person, I will not hesitate to come unglued.

All the ones who saw my love.
All the ones whom I gave a fuck.
Especially if I made it clear, tore my bloody beating heart to show.
As they impaled it with spears, buried under stone.
I'm fucking done, I'm out for blood, turning tables without fear.

Waited since ten, depression made me impaired.
Knew it was coming, Satan trained my soul.
But I'm lashing out; I'm fucking done with this self control.
I'll bleed if I want, you cunts matter no more.
I'll take my life when I feel it's time to pass forth.
I gave it my best, but nothing worked out.
Blood soaked pentagram drawn on the floor.
Save me now or enjoy the self-destructive show.

Tired of forcing myself to go along.
Tired of making excuses for things gone wrong.
The pain inflicted onto my ratchet soul.
So, to the goat, Satan's steed: do you hear my call?
I have nothing left inside me that wants to fight it down.
Face me, Hades, you miserable God of underground.
I'm here, I hear you are the one who damned my soul.
Blood soaked arms; this is the fight to fucking win them all!

Under Construction

Between the phases beside my other half, trying to get out.
Critical and full of judgments, wanting to lash out.
Other side of the pendulum swings to the caring me.
Constant battle between him and the evil me.

Tell me of misfortune and so-called luck.
The whispers in my ear tell me to ask, "why did you fuck up?"
Tell me of the things that broke or the anger you inflict.
It whispers back at me to ask, "why are you such a prick?"

Normally I would assume they cause all their own pain.
I mean, it's fairly obvious how easy that would be.
Normally I'd just tell it how I see but seems to me that lately, I don't listen to that me.

See, I noticed something within the past few weeks.
That when I'm dealing with my shit and I begin to suffocate.
When I need a friend or to feel someone gives a shit about me.
I tend to become over positive and I over care.

When I feel I may not see another day.
When the taunting in my head wants to kill the pain.
I reciprocate, hoping it comes back.
I try and be the better than average version of myself.
I hope that it cancels out that burning destructive need.
But as the words leave this vessel, I get a little angry.

I want to be the balance of both of my ways.
If someone says something stupid, I'd point it out right away.
If someone bitches about a problem they never should have had.

The real me would more than likely laugh.
Not that I don't give a shit, but that you brought it to yourself.

Ask what you expected, and if you're happy with how things turned out.
Why is it that the best you got, seems lazy as can be?
Maybe if you gave a fuck, you would set yourself free.
Self created problems because you don't deserve.
I think it's time you sat the fuck down and looked back into the mirror.

Point out what went wrong and also what is going right.
Not be so soft and light with my insight.
That's the real me underneath this crap.
But I know what I give out is set to come back.
My days haven't been so good, but they don't have a clue.
No one bothers to fucking ask, so no one knows the truth.

This is the habit developed by the craft.
Before, I used to lash out.
I was too harsh at best.
I'd make people feel useless.
Tell them to their face.
But that same energy, back to me, it came.
So now I'm torn between this and the evil me.
Trying to find a balance and not seem so grossly clean.
Maybe I should say fuck it and just go back to my old me.

I know my strengths and where I am weak.
I know being too supportive can seem too fake.
I see how I tend to ignore myself and miscalculate.
What first pops up hasn't been what I say.
Because I see that it is driving me insane.

So, I'm trying really hard to reconstruct a better way.
To call them out but not push them away.
Cause I'm black and white; a lot of what I can say is brutal and overkill, and not
what I want to be.
Guess I'll test the waters and see how I can mix the two me's.
So, fuck you, but have a nice day.

Intuitive Psychic

Touched on a subject and hinted of love.
I barely scratched the surface, and that was hard enough.
Gave rope to run with, but not enough to kill.
Tried to keep it subtle but show how much I care.

Touched on the subject, given half control.
Either everything changes or nothing, nothing at all.
Everything changes or nothing at all.
I see you in my mind, your voice is locked inside.
I see you in my dreams, your presence stained my soul.
I open up like a book, dusty pages and torn.
If you clean them off, you will find it written in a language unknown.

Hinted at love but possibly I failed.
I want to be there when you win, frown and smile.
But these visions haunt my brain.
I'm trying to change the channel.
They come in waves, straight from hell.
I see glimpses of what could never be forgotten.

There's a chance that it's just my mind.
Just my brain being creative.
There is a chance that nothing will ever happen.
But what I've been shown is the last nail in the coffin.
What my visions are holding, your timeline has already proven.
I must be a piece of shit for this to happen.
There is a chance I'll go multiple years locked inside my dungeon.
Like 7.5 billion but you're the only person.
I wonder what is wrong with me.
As I except inevitable rejection, cause sometimes forgiveness can't be given.
Play with fire when you play with my emotions.

Especially after all of the conversations.
Just because I would sacrifice my health, doesn't mean you get forgiveness.
There is a fine line and a big difference.
I was available, you weren't, and it wasn't spite driven.
Shit wasn't a plan in the making.
Vindictive is a childish excuse, not a fucking reason.

I said it since the fucking beginning, you can't pull that shit and expect me to not take it personal.
You gonna leave me with no choice now.
I had to cancel the subscription.
You say you care but no, not feeling the connection.

Take care, I'll be off in the distance.
Maybe in another life, in another dimension.
The timing just ain't right, I'm running from emotion.

I tore down my walls and that wasn't worth even a conversation.
I fucking did what kills me most, but I get it, it was my own decision.
Guess it's the crossroads now, guess it's time for division.
Birds of a feather but I don't fuck with a pigeon.
Treat me like shit, knowing I'm prone to depression.
Your trying to push me to kill myself, while you sit back and smile.
You want to see the knife slide down these arms just to feel something.
You've proven you hate me; I'm not staying for a revision.
Fuck you; I'm a piece of shit but you're on a lower level.
Fuck you, fuck your lies, fuck your sob stories and fuck you for even breathing.

After all the time and energy I have given.
After all the energy you have stolen.
After everything I told you about what I can't stand in a human.
You turn around and purposefully do it?
Why? What was the reason? You needed to feel even? You personalised something that had nothing to do with you.
You stooped to a level lower than the shit I'm shoveling.
This whole time was all for nothing.
This was a crime and its punishment is a life sentence.
You can't fucking lie to an intuitive psychic.
Who the fuck do you think you are?
Fuck you are stupid!

Subliminal Truth of Humanity

This goes out to you all who have bled to feel, who have opened themselves up and became someone's joke.

This is a shout out to all who ask themselves why, why do I continue to breathe when true peace is when you die?

I relate to the stereotypical groups named Emo and Goth, I periodically loop from happy to not.

Perhaps if I couldn't see or think as deeply, I too would remain stuck in happy.

Perhaps if schools' curriculum had worked, my depressive reality would have not left me broken down and drowsy.

To all those that say they understand, I'd like to slit their throats, serrated blade in hand.

Fuck you, you preps have not a fucking clue.

If you felt what I feel, you'd be found strung up in a noose.

Its sickening to hear day in and day out that this medication is fake, and the disease is a joke.

That we just feel sorry for ourselves and choose to live in this drought.

Accusations placed by beings with no clue, never holding the blade soaked in their own DNA.

Blood running down to the floor asking once more should I try this again or just end the game?

Suicide is engraved inside and the stupidity of my peers, fucking intolerant queers, give up your complex and get over your fears.

Makes me want to end this existence even more.

Perhaps its time you put the drugs down and clear your mind to realize you too are medicating to escape the now.

Ingestion of substance with no nutritional value is a means of escaping the fucking world around you.

Stop lying to yourself and just do it already, slit your own throat this place doesn't need you.

All you fucking self righteous finger pointing sluts, it is you whom I don't give a fuck.

There's more thinking and remembering of bad than good.

We're focusing on reliving the problems like crime in the hood.

If all of our minds were opened to the level some have reached there would be no need, no reason for all that is preached.

It feels as though it's our morals that we need to feed, to grow and learn but instead we get high and breed.

The disgust of who we have become will cut you deep, make the truth leak.

The wounds of life are comparably bleak and the stain is on our skin as though we permanently bleed.

Wash it away with honesty and truth but you can't because you're weak.

Pull it together, make it count this time spent is short such as last week, just a memory left in some and lost in others because time wasted is bittersweet.

Living this life to the fullest extent, governed only by the cards in which we're dealt.

Use the knowledge in which some time was spent, not well but gone.

For ever so make peace, remember the things it taught.

It's the way it is, has and always will be.

Sometimes life is cruel, mixed up with ruthless and criminally insane but who are you to judge because you know your own pain, weakness and unguarded terrain.

We are all imperfect and fucked if you will, one small piece of one big pot of fucked up humanity is disgusting and I include myself in this all.

But fuck it tomorrow is another day just like the last, one foot in front of the other until we pass.

I'm a Loser

It echoes like the madness, like it's all I know.
I'm a let down, sweetie, it's the story untold.
I have been fighting a war and growing cold.
I've been through hell so many times, I have my own floor.
I have blood on my hands from the hearts I've broken.
I have blood on my hands, decapitated corpses of the people I've known.

I'm not surprised at the neglect for myself.
I've been running them circles, ravens overhead.
I'm not surprised at the neglect I get.
I have so much karma, hon, and that bitch never forgets.

I'm a let down, a fuck up and toxic at best.
I'm trying to be good, but the past never forgets.
I'm not surprised I've maintained this level of being hated.
I can't say I blame the general public.
I count my blessings as I gasp and spit.
I choke on my pride with every breath I took.
I'm a loser and I'm not proud of it.
I'm a loser and I'm not proud of it.
If I were you, I'd bite, chew and spit me out.
What worth can I have with a past so dark?
What does it matter if I'm doing my part?
I'm gonna fail at the one thing we want.
I'm a let down, sweetie, that's all you get.

One line from a song that made them famous.
I plagiarized the palisades.
Cause I'm a let down, hon, it's what you get.
No matter how I try and rewrite it.

I failed them hard, I'm a piece of shit.
Lost in myself, locked like a skeleton in that dusky closet.

I fucked up my name cause I'm a piece of shit.
I fail at the game cause my conscious relives it.
They all left me because I'm fucking useless.
I wont wrap that shit nicely; I'm a piece of shit.
They raped every emotion I had left.
Fueled with hatred for everything that I am.

I try and I try to recover from it.
I bend and I contort, trying to fit.
But I'm a let down and we both know it.
Hon, I'm a fuck up and I know it.

I'm useless and I'm never gonna fit.
I'm a loser and I'm not proud of it.
I'm a loser and I'm not proud of it.
I'm a loser and I'm not proud of it.
I break my back every chance that I get.
I tried harder for you than I ever will admit.

I'd give my life for a chance to rewrite.
I'd slit my throat for a new insight.
But I'm nothing, if not a piece of shit.
I'm a let down and everyone knows it.
I fight it off the best I can.
I beg and barter with the wraith of time.
I cut the deals with Satan himself.
I'd give this soul of it wasn't useless.
I'd take all your pain and leave you in peace.
I'm a let down but that's not my intent.
I'm a loser, hon, and I'm not proud of it.

Restless Nights, Irrational Mind-Talk

Questions and confusion of what truly is.

Delusions of a pattern, lifestyle that breaks my inner being.

Conclusion not come to, for trust has been broken.

Solutions to this issue are simple, subtle and needed.

Questions in my head screaming and shouting, beliefs of honesty, the one thing in which I'm deserving.

Border line catastrophe, internally I am bleeding.

Questions in my mind, for in ignorance is bliss?

These emotions intertwined with my ability to forgive.

In love and possibly blind, my heart is begging for us to live.

Answers I'll find, for in time it all comes around.

Just remember to unwind and let destiny run its course.

Though honestly, its honesty that will make us live, painful it may be, but the truth is what a decent person gives.

The Story of James

Three years he hasn't said a word
Cheap threats made
Guess the crystal really took control

He came home after work to her clothes scattered on the ground
He's seen this all before
The self destruction of a once loved one

Felt the stitching of his soul tearing at the seems
The voices in his head lashing out again
Always treated like dirt, you deserve it
Always deceived, too nice, it's too easy
Can't take it anymore
Everyone just up and leaves him

Two weeks pass
He was dead inside
Skipping out on work
Skipping out on life
Two weeks passed, he died on the inside

Another week went on
Text showed up, sent from her to him
Says she's pregnant and she claims it's his
Red flags cause he found out she was hooking on the side
Just like that, the questions got shined with light

The next few weeks, they all seemed so grey
In the end of it all, this is what she had to say:
"It's my body, its my baby. I do what I see fit and you're gonna have no part. I'll
make sure of it!"

Her mother sent a message backing up all of it
He is not a part of the picture, will have nothing to do with it
Said its over, there's no need to talk
Nothing left to explain
Just like that, he was ghosted, completely ignored and drained

So, he slowly drifts away into the corners of his mind
He faded out inside, he really crossed a line
He had no choice if he had a chance to survive
He had not a single friend that would have helped him fight in the end

And the threats made were clear, she had an army at her side, backed by that
crystal drug life

So, he numbed himself; he killed the heart within his chest
He was done with this
Worked, trying to pay off debt
He dreamed about his life and the ways he would end it
Kill off the pain inside, feelings can't be mended

Been three years now, he's tired and wants to go back home
Home to the place underneath the tree
Home is where he will swing alone
Kicked out stool underneath

Then just the other day, another message received
Genetics came back
Guess it really is his kid
Same thing though, he will have no say in it

He grips the knife again as he carves into his own flesh
Want to feel a pain that is different
Have no words left, no love that he can give
All he knows is he is going to end it

He doesn't get it, what's the point of telling all of this?
You all threw him to the wolves
Now what? He's just supposed to give a shit.
Three years killing off what's inside

Three years, it's way too late
Tomorrow he will be dead
Supported flesh
The gravitational finish
What else is left when nothing sticks?

Me vs Me

Evil comes in different forms, demons that linger and plague the soul.
It's something that steals from me each day.
I fight with it internally, presenting externally, an unbearable frown.
Even when I do feel happy and remember what I have, it never really brightens or
portrays that side of this man.
It whispers in my ear, exhaling its infectious cold, dense air.
Torments the mind and brings up stories of the past.
I fight and I try to ignore it and live on, medication is what my life has become.
Doctors call it a disease and offer so many pills, while the patient is dying and
being overcome with fears.
My tormentor is wicked, smart and truly doesn't care; he comes out from hiding
when I let my guard down, almost a test or challenge you unwillingly pursue.
He derails my feelings and turns love into pain, makes me feel unworthy, like I'm
holding people down.
I battle back inside my wicked mind, an arena where I have previously drowned.
Upon such battles my being looks sad; some even feel like they always make
me mad.
I am exhausted and mentally stressed, I also see both these people, the warrior
and restless.
And I scream from the sidelines ' what the fuck are you doing? You're going to
wreck this!'.
All these things, day in and day out, help as much as I can before my times up.
I blame myself and this disease for taking from me all the things I deserve, but do
I really if it's myself I blame?

Talking to Myself

Branded with the word welcome on my being, a door mat is how I'm feeling.
Footprints left on my face; this is my story and I must embrace.
Left for another not once, not twice, but thrice
Tortured soul, bleeding and weeping.
Creating new scars, for all I know is bleeding.
Years of built anticipation, lied to and stomped on; how the fuck is it still beating?
I am the best person I know.
The rest of you are full of lies with hearts of coal.
This is not worth the pain at all; my minds made up, it's not my fault.
Love is stronger than heroin and I'm pushing an overdose.
Arms remain open, blood is flowing adjacent the shards of the mirror on the
concrete bathroom floor.
The pain inside haunts me at night.
I'm afraid of letting anyone know what I plan.
No one to care, there's literally no one here.
So much effort and pride to build a life to share and left with not a single care.
I'm aware of so much more than I let on but it's trust that I give and you've got
it all.
Its love that I have and you are the only one to see it entrapped behind my wall.
I love me and I'm the best person I know.
Suicide is properly executed internally.
My soul.
Life of abuse and its ok, I'm used.
Mean nothing to no one and that's ok, I guess I'm worthless after all.
I always try and fight my internal demons on my own.
I'm a piece of shit to you all, I've been made to know.
Not worth a breath taken from an infected lung.
It's my life's half willingly sung song.
I vent to myself and you read and judge as you please, not actually knowing what's
inside me.

A New Movement

On the edge of awakening no longer walking in this hell we fear.
The verge of passing through my devils' door to create a mess and take control.
I'm walking the ledge and glancing out; I'm here for a fight so get the fuck up!

Get the fuck up and push through the fears; face those demons today is our day.
Darkness can be enlightened and wounds will heal, so pick yourself up and join the movement.
Get the fuck up! We can push through this
Get the fuck up! You know you can do it

Find our souls and take the long way home, save what's left and build it back up for tonight its going down.
This life is a nightmare and torments are all that's known but we're changing our ways and leaving the flames.
Drowning is a feeling similar to breathing and the water is murky poison leached from treason.
Half the pain is believing, this is not a reason for repetitive bleeding.
The shards of what was taught fit together if you build on it.

So just get the fuck up and look around, notice the world's in pain and you aren't alone.
See so much shame displayed in crooked frames.
Get the fuck up, get the fuck up and get the fuck out.

Lessons Learned

In the past, what feels like so long ago; I was in a place, dark with no hope.
In those days so very grim, I let myself down and inherited guilt within.
I lived a lie and let the darkness consume me; I was at a loss and anyone could woo me.
I betrayed myself and took part in a nasty lie.
It didn't have to happen, I can't imagine why or how I could become so lost, so heartless and impure.
I held a hatred, a guilt I'll never forget; I was in shambles and losing my grip.
Then around the time I was counting my loss, I acquired some conversation from a friend long lost.
Through the jokes and the laughter, the dialogue would always change, through this digital communication I felt something worth saving, that my soul I could maintain.
I knew what I had to do but didn't harbor the courage, knew what I felt but feared I was delirious.
I pondered and slept on it for nights come and gone.
Till the option I had was no longer around.
I swore to myself to redeem my old morals; I promised myself I was truly not that person.
The days moved on and the time finally came, I had been handed my karma on a silver plate.
I spent a year and a half rebuilding my being.
I hate what I've done, and I remember that shitty feeling, it's with this haunted memory in which I've remained clean.
No longer a person who doesn't think about anyone else, no longer resentful of humans them self.
In life we make mistakes and we can choose to learn, if you're smart enough to recognize that what you've done is wrong then your smart enough to leave that part of you behind in the dirt where it belongs.

I believe people can change and I speak from experience, that's why I don't hold anger and resentment. Instead I offer forgiveness.

We all make a mistake, we all have done wrong but that's part of learning and development of the soul.

Offered Opinion

Holding on by a dream of life, falling away from the accumulation of dark insight.
Get through the days that seem to drag on and open those eyes, acknowledge what is going on.
Listen to the whispers carried freely in the breeze.
There are messages to be heard as the wind rushes through the trees.
Holding heads in hands so beaten.
Tortures of the soul whose body is weakened.
These years go on and lessons will be learned but what do you do when it becomes a chore just to remain breathing?
Occasionally plagued with the feeling that this life may be worth leaving.
It's the light in the dark that we're seeing.
A flicker of hope to keep heavy hearts in rhythm and beating.
The gift of knowing of awareness and freedom, sometimes wears you out.
Seriously, I'm not kidding.
Try as we do and come as you are because at the end of the day we have often gone too far.
To error is human and human we shalt be, subconsciously connected to the universe, indeed.

A Text to Dad

Sorry, I'm so distant
It's hard cause I feel like quitting.
I know I'm far from perfect, but I know that I am gifted.
I feel so much sorrow.
I feel like, for years I tried to follow.
I admire who you are;
my father, my friend,
my brightest star.
I look at you and ponder
the long nights, the lost days,
all the time you spent away,
the ulcers and unrequited depression.
You know, I know you can't go through that without breaking.
So, this is for the lost tears, the fears, and all of your ambition.
I do try but I can't cry, the tears for me are frozen.
I love you; I love all your lessons.
I approach life with you in mind and I just want to be a blessing.
But, this new news of my bullshit life unfolding;
Its been a pill I just can't swallow.
No words left, no need for conversation.
Nothing will suffice and words will darken my depression.
Bare with me, Dad, just know I was in observation.
All your hard work and love spilled for a family, for granted you are not taken.
Give me time, please.
Too many decisions I am making.
I love you.

Dim Lit Days

Sick and in silence, feels like breathing in ashes, pulse of the people whose words are weapons.

Did it ever occur that without words, you're useless?

Take part in this play as the character of your choosing; Destiny is a bitch, for I now get why everyone is using.

The never-ending attempt to be all you feel you can, but how's that gonna work when, from your conscience you have ran?

People come and people go but it's people who created this beauty within the living hell.

I stand here to bid you the kindest farewell.

Stand, I do and choke me it might, but it's my life and for acceptance I won't fight.

The intuitions are there, anyone can tap into it; they're being pulled from thin air.

Listen to the voice, the feeling in your gut and put down the finger which points to another for blame.

It's lazy, childish and shows a lot of your fears.

Honesty and kindness, two traits for the wisest.

Empty promises and half ass lying, traits of those whom live in the closets, sheltered from reality with spirits, moth eaten.

Perhaps it's a perspective, just another asshole who seems to be prejudice.

Maybe the pain of a mind so over worked has left this individual subconsciously lost in the dark.

What if it's the scars left on such a kind heart that turn blank pages into lyrical messes?

More to ponder and lost in wonder, plagued with this gift and subconsciously throwing a fit.

Guess this is it just another passage from a guy whose mind and soul successfully co exist.

Thinking

Like winds through a desert, my thoughts race and erode away little parts of me.
Times I spend vacant inside the shell of my sanity, provide me with an honest
perspective of this disastrous reality.

Slowly drifting in and out of actuality, processing each moment individually.
What if I hadn't gone this way? What if I caved to the evil in me?
How the strings of fate are woven has picked at my curiosity.

There's a plan, you see, it's preordained and built-in genetically.
To sit and cry and keep asking why, searching for an answer or screaming out
towards the sky
creates emotions that are completely unnecessary.

Time won't wait for you but will you wait on time?
Life is about giving in to time, expressing ourselves and enjoying the ride.

No One

Are you doing fine? Just rhetorical questions and no answer will suffice.
Sitting inside that protective bubble.
Your tainted sense of pride.
I watch from across the other side.
As the rain changes the tide, amongst the rubble, nothing can hide.

Are you doing fine?
Haven't heard a word since the beginning of the last time.
Will it be a substitute for just alright?
Will silence break?
Or will it continue to rain all night?
Will silence break?
Is there anything left inside?

Programmed for self destruction, the game is slowing down.
Programmed by deception, its left a cold inside.
As you stood by my side and deceived me for the last time.
Are you ok? As you slid the knife within my spine.
Look unto my eyes and watch the tide pull me out again.

Silence speaks more than ever before.
The disgust of this race.
The permanent bitter taste of all that never was.
The hatred has now been fed.
Should I even try?
Try to contain it.

Will it be a substitute for just alright?
Will silence break?
Or will it continue to rain all night?

Will silence break?
Will it break?
Will there be a return of your light?

Days feel like hours and time is on my side.
I can already smell the flowers.
Rotting outside.
Hours, now like minutes.
My shadows left my side.
New found emptiness, in the rain, drowning in the riptide.

Will it be a substitute for just alright?
Will silence break?
Or will it continue to rain all night?
Will silence break?
Will the loneliness subside?
Feels like forever since my words dissipated.
Nothing seems to come out right.
Ruptured mind, wasteland of today.
So, I tell another lie and say I am alright.
So, I play this sick game.
The opposite of what is inside.

No one understands.
No one by my side.
Words are nothing when slipped from serpent's twisted tongue.
No one understands.
But ya, I will be alright.
Will they understand when I leave to the otherside?

Will it be a substitute for just alright?
Will silence break?
Or will it continue to rain all night?
Will silence break?
Will it break before I break for the other side?
Will silence break? I just want a break.
If only for tonight.

Your Power, My Treason

Dream of demons, friends of darkness.
Familiar faces, haunting spaces.
Mind's a big mess and inside I am pacing.
Dreams of demons choking me, until abruptly I awaken.

These dreams are timeless.
I made it on the spiritual hit list.
But demons are best friends.
Keep me humble, remind me I am worthless.
Dreams of demons reminding me where my place is.

The rope has already been hanging.
Eight knots deep, not a single breath's escaping.
Life for a life is a blessing.
To restart in a different direction.
No more living in comparison.
No more double standards placed by a lesser human.

Stalking me like I'm a specimen.
Diverting life experience because of a twisted vision.
Demons looking better than the most beautiful woman.
Not a practice of malice, just an old tradition.

I see and I feel what has only been written.
The crafted path of my short existence.
I've accomplished more with less opportunity given.
Blocked an aspect of how I could be living.
But now I'm on a different mission.
Hearts in cages, that's a given.
I had the choice, but I chose no fucks given.

Come out of the shadows.
Come out into the picture.
Trust in me when I offer something different.
What I have to give is but a lesson.
Dreams of demons, their powers at my disposal.
Not a practice of malice, but an old tradition.

Set the mirror to reflect what has been given.
Let the refraction steal for you what was unlawfully taken.
Set the fire of the darkest ambitions.
Terminated contracts with my place you are taking.

Now cut the chords of deception.
Cut all ties with no chance of reconnection.
With these mirrors, I cancel your subscription.
I call upon the demons to withstand a resurrection.

Dreams of demons, the friends in my corner.
Dance within darkness and learn to live all over.
Dreams of demons, no power could hold me.
So, to you I send them running.

Nameless

Signal the sirens, songs of silence.
Pencil this sketch, an image of darkness.
Delusions of cruelness granted with kindness.

Deception between this is life in dissection.
Haunting the mind like a knife holding your own reflection.

The beauty within this is lost to self-negligence; neglect is why we all walk a wreck.

Paths through the gates of our own personal hell, torture's the test that builds the character that forms when all is stripped from the hands of the deserving.

There is beauty placed in the hands of the unworthy, while the rest fight just to remain breathing.

Morning Conversation with Myself

When patience wears thin and the cords of deception penetrate the skin.
When the sickness within builds and provides fuel to the demon's kiln.
For in this moment, it's best for all to retreat into the abyss, to cut ties with the world in which summoned, this soon-to-be violent mess.

Patience is a gift and some have been spoiled, re thinking whom deserves and who doesn't care.
I see more than presented and know more than I have been taught.
Spreading acceptance and accepting negligence leaves the body, mind and soul curious as to where the fuck to go.
There's the path less followed and the path of least resistance.

I make the path for myself and it runs jagged through the forest.
All are welcome, though no one's here; story of that patience is something that I fear.
It's a test of time and its crossing that line, take a step back and deep breathe.
Today I will not let you see, tomorrow I could be free.

Often thoughts bring the question of tomorrow with only knowledge of the past.
When patience wears thin you will be empty within.
To be at peace in mind, in this moment in time is a gift I'm willingly taking.
To accept your flaws and cherish who you are is a goal worth chasing.
You will never come up short, no defeat can be obtained.
In the end its you, my friend, who has all the answers.

Learn about who you are with constructive self analyzation.
Think back on the days and those choices you've made and I'm sure you will see a connection.
The patterns are there hiding in thin air, nothing but a perfect reflection.

It's not the mistakes, the hardships and restraints of the past which defines us, the knowledge we gain and even the pain is meant to teach us a lesson.

Not out of spite or karma and her nasty bite, but through a bigger connection.
Whatever you believe, just know that things do happen for a reason.
Live for yourself but don't forget about everyone else and be true to your conscious.
It's a journey we're on and we're all gonna be fine, mostly because it's my friends who can read this.

A Martyr

Is this my world, a place to live?
Will this be the best I get?
Awake and walking, think I'm losing grip.
Is this my world?
No alternate.

The path paved easy.
Trampled by the sheep.
The trail of resistance.
Runs adjacent, narrow and steep.

My map is crimson.
Stained from the blood of my wrist.
So, my path is unrelenting.
Runs jagged through the woods.

Through tormented valleys.
Over icy peaks.
Lost in forever.
Until the river six, calm water at my feet.
Like a Phoenix from deaths ashes.
A new perspective calls to me.

The journey is all but over.
Stitch the wounds up nice and neat.
Perhaps I have to suffer.
A martyr of the sheep.
Write scriptures for tomorrow.
As roses wilt under feet.

An empath with a gift.
I steal all your pain.
Spill it onto paper, words that I see fit.
A gift to you from me?
Is this curse in fact a gift?

I wrote this in response to a whisper. Shall call it "Theft of a Gift"

When you view yourself as shit, but the world sees potential
It makes it hard to push forward because you have plagued your own mind with thoughts that are evil.
It won't matter what is said or what is left unspoken; as soon as you realise it's you that is keeping yourself broken.
Doesn't matter the colour or build of the being.
After all, we are limited to the amount of time we remain breathing.
You probably aren't perfect, and you know all your own flaws, but have you accepted that you can shape who you are?
Appreciate the little things like the birds and the trees.
Notice it's imperfection that makes us unique.
For there is no ugly, no not at all.
Because with 6 billion people there is admiration for all!
All builds, all colours, even psychopaths too.
We all have someone who loves us no matter what we do.
So next time you see your own reflection, as hard as it may be
Find at least one feature of your being to be grateful for and you will see.
In time, after practice and believing in yourself, you will overcome this feeling of self-doubt.

Day Dream

All these lyrics flowing in my mind leaving reality vague, distant, unrefined.
Knowing not where they come from, feeling arrhythmic heart beats timed.
Words with such power, lost grace and raw hope in relieving is a passage
Lost ink from my pen upon this open book.
I could do this for hours, weaving thought into words but it's like weeding
flowers, exhausting on the mind when you're lacking descriptive words.
Sit and stare at paper and let these lines come pouring out; I should have warned
you early that I feel emotions fully, just not how you think, no doubt.
I sit and ponder for hours, think about how life's turned out.
Relive some treasured moments lost in the vault of my mind like a drought of
peaceful decisions made that I couldn't live without.
I sit with a mind that's active but it's not all that bad.
So long as I have me controlled; acknowledge but calmly walk away.
Its not the light that's shining, it's the one that slipped away for I look into my
eyes and see room for one more flame.

Approach Me

Talk to me; let me know I'm somewhat worthy.

Confide in me and grant me just a portion of your time, it's not much, really.

Approach me; tell me the things that you're holding from me.

Communication is key and, if not established, leaves a presumptuous label: Vanity.

Call me, text me, tell me you think of me.

I'm not giving into this distance of reality.

Show me; prove to me that I'm not just another fucking nobody.

Ask me questions about me, come on and get the whole story.

Approach me, sit down for some coffee; I bet you try me and find you can confide in me.

Test me not likely, for playing games is not exciting; be real with me and peak me spiritually, let the words of truth come out as you can open up to me but first, I need you to approach me.

I've spent my time, more years than you can hide

Been through the getting over of my pride because I'm no longer hiding what's inside.

My value is greater than any money can buy and I'm not about numbers, I don't let age plague my mind I'm about reality and I won't tolerate lies, so just approach me.

Facades

Wrong side of the bed, I awoke in a dream.
The facade of you there, why did you reach for me?
One body drowning as another jumps in.
The water has no more tension.
Together, we fight for air.

You matched my vibrations and pulled me to the shore.
We matched in scars; in body, not soul.
A victim of pills, prescriptions sent to take control.

Often, I wonder: were we ever friends?
Often, I doubted, you must have subliminal plans.
I ignored my depression and focused on you.
I lit the torch of your psyche and told the stories, explained the tangible truths.

I ignored the whispers, my intuitive ways.
I tricked myself and believed all of your claims.
I sat and I listened to every word you would say.
I bit my tongue as your actions betrayed.

Contradictive was a word best used to describe.
All your little rants turned into half baked lies.
All my prior visions turned out to be right.
No one is perfect but all I asked was to try.

Hollows of the Mind

Fog in the streets and mist in the mind, a delusion of friends with lies intertwined.
Lost and in shambles, in shadows, dying inside.
Truth is going nowhere and nothing passes the time.

Fog in the streets, every corner in the mind, lay dormant under sheets and giving up inside.
Tournament of ghosts, demons aren't confined.
Play with emotions and stir up memories, past lives.

Know not what is needed but exceeded intellect of wasted time.
Life makes not a sense nor a spark of dim light; coma carries over when rest is death locked inside.
Give up, beautiful person, for distress leaves you tired; paralyzed is the body but awake in twisted minds.

Courage to explore further and discover jesters with crooked smiles.
Plead for understanding but get tossed to the side, rejection of our angels can destroy all of our pride.
Frost in the mountains, the tasks too hard to climb.
Bring out strength unknown because you're dying inside.
Hold hands with the demons as evil fills the inside, fires of broken palaces turning dreams to dust in no time.

Give in to darkness right before your shown the light; it's a promise because patience has died.
Fog fills the streets and seeps into weak minds, confide in arch angels and to your feet may you rise.
Spill the blood of the evil, entities that cannot fight.
Decapitated strangers, burn bodies with fierce light.

Line hallways with bodies, hang the unworthy from skylight.
Pray on weakness, leaving no survivors in sight.
Murder the dark deceivers, skin them all alive.
Bring on foggy walkways, its time to stand and fight.

Fog in the streets and mist in the mind, a delusion of friends with lies intertwined.
Lost and in shambles, in shadows dying inside.
Truth is going nowhere and nothing passes the time.

Fog in the streets, every corner in the mind
Lay dormant under sheets and giving up inside.
Tournament of ghosts, demons aren't confined.
Play with emotions and stir up memories, past lives.

Obscure Observation

Simple solutions, producing multiple delusions; the system of life is rigged.
For wrong is only perceived by those in dire need, to re connect to the light.
Though unfortunately a lot of humans can't see what lies beyond their eyesight,
because in reality, it's not what can be seen that brings purpose to our life.

Living locked away within our own bone cage is not what it should be about.
Living carefree in a peaceful harmony, existing purely in loving energy, should be
the stage of our life.
Though it seems selfish, dreams and neglect produce an intoxicating side effect.
Chasing those dreams, made up of nothing, serving no purpose but to your own
delusional game
Living this life, working out of spite, breaking time to do some wrong.

I see it everyday, all over this place we live amongst the hurt and low self esteem.
It's not what you've been given, but what you can do for the people around you
because we are all on the same team.
I'm a human too, though I see it in my own point of view, it doesn't change this
connection and I'm not ashamed.
I guess some have no clue and that's ok too, I guess not everyone has an open
brain.
Some think their so smart and play with ill art, but that's ok, next round will
surely take care of you.
For I hold no hate, though I do know my place, I will not tolerate the fake I'll live
in peaceful solitude.
I'm here in plain sight, arms open wide to just a few; you know who you are
because you haven't done me wrong, just showed who you are as we've shared a
memory or two.
I don't work out of spite or tie into dark light, because I'm better than those
who do.
I'm open to explain and possibly express pain when the time has become due.

Life is almost a game and cheating is just insane, creating hamsters caught in a loop.

The people of this time need to remind and observe what they have been up to. Seriously, it's not hard to see where we fell apart and take a note or two.

Change the approach, don't fall victim to comfort zones; seriously, just try something new.

Don't whine and complain, your keeping yourself in the rain, though amusing from another point of view.

Chasing cmotion by indulging in substance is something we don't need to do. Numbing some pain, that's an excuse that's maintained by recreating your day; literally, just stuck in your loop.

Give it some thought: are you doing your part in reinventing a greater you? Guess its too hard so just stay how you are, cause that's obviously all you let yourself do.

Untitled

In sickness and health, plagued with visions straight from hell.
Darkness condensed in wealth, blood stained minds encased like waters in a well.
See the plague lives in us all, momentarily derailed by whispers from the dark occult.
The darkness balances us all, denying it is supplying the curse.
Similar to "dropping the ball"
Does this mean you live in hell?

No it means we be both, angels fallen and part crawling from the gates of hell.
Think this passage is wrong?
Take a look on your life, replay all those shady songs.
Embrace this blackened fractured heart or repair and turn to light, it's your call.
Fractured pictures falling from shaken walls, the story is forever changing, those readings will prove to be wrong.

Sickness healed from interior health, confused coherency will topple the beast, good lives in us all.
Release us from unscripted hell.
Call it a satanic ball, standing here ringing satans twisted bell.
Call out to tortured souls, tempting black magic's practices of the lesser occult.
Call it what it is.
Impractical practice of malice.
Witches of agony living amongst us, it's a free for all.

Minds molded how you want it, follow and you will see a craft to persuade negative energy.
Deflection of reflections not serving purpose in this conspiracy.
Acknowledge the darkness, minds cloudy conflicted hypocrisy from wall to wall.
Pray for plagues that end this all.
Pray for graves, darkness' funeral.

But pray for grace, for the ability to win the race.
Running, escaping out pacing probable fates.
Pray for voice, you have it but using it's a personal choice.
It's the strings of fate, truth is, you actually have a say.
Speak up or lose your place, become invisible in silence.
A ghost haunting usable space.
Listen to the whispers from within the neglected place, Pandora's Box buried
inside the valley of mistakes.

Quick breath because quick left; now struggles with slow reflection stuck on
repeat.
Sit back and swallow pride that kept you from a happy retreat.
Kick back and relax while life is stuck on repeat, blackness again plagues the brain
as you live in your self inflicted defeat.

Welcome back the land of the black, comfort soon betrays.
Welcome black, the colour reflecting your shady ways.
Get it back and leave the pack, don't be afraid.
Come back and stand up, make it your day.
Be fast and dodge past, end the masquerade.

Reflections

Where once lived a dream, a program I designed to live happy and free.
Where once I had a team, a group of people who always seemed to be around me.
When once I was actually free, not corrupt with this awkward dark obscenity.

Feels like I slept in and missed the test, I'm out here left of center at best.
Absent minded, mistaken for clinically depressed, often times I'm misunderstood cause often my lines are dark, crude or a mess.
Lots of times writing about blood painted rooms, bathroom floors scattered with limbs and bodies hanging from a fucking noose.
Writing about times that never existed, making shit up because it's intriguingly twisted.
Learned early on that none of this means shit, I've always been looked at like I'm fucking different.

Where once was a dream, a program of my own design, now lays in ashes inside my tangled mind.
Where once was hope and smiles and pride, now is self motivation and my own fucking shadow that helps me pass the time.
When once I felt like a part of a team is now a reality that nothing living actually wants to hang around me.

Feelings used to fucking plague me, confused and distracted by lies that my teachers gave me.
Corrupt in the mind because I called out all the bullshit, labeled whatever from people who don't stand for shit.
Time I always seem to waste it, I showed you who I am and got tossed to the side without a bat of the eye cause I'm just a disposable piece of shit, so fuck it.
I write about bleach that I swallow in gulps and about skinning bodies of victims and such.
I write like I have no spark, like I have nothing left, not even a heart.

I'm a monster, a beast, a depressed fucking freak; that weirdo, that clown, the loser with a frown.

I'm not saying it from truth, I'm repeating others points of view, for I'm not fucking deaf or a fool and ya I do know more than you.

No, I'm not gay but I've been called a fag and no, I'm not mental or ill in the head, I'm just an example of what happens when a child's left for dead.

Been told that I'm ugly, that my purpose I don't serve, asked to kill myself for the air I breathe is a waste of health and I don't deserve it.

Sometimes I feel I'm stuck in hell but that doesn't make me less or not well.

Some days I just lay in bed wishing, hoping, praying I woke up dead.

Life in its whole has been a fucking struggle I'll never forget; my childhood was missing; I searched every mile before I gave up.

My teenage years never fucking happened, I grew up overnight it was a fucking disaster.

Plagued with dreams I never repeat, learning answers to questions that no one could teach.

Meetings with shrinks left wanting more, could see I baffled them all as I walked out their door.

Visions of life and wanting to end it, knowing too much I couldn't just forget it.

You see depression and agony, I see intellect and pain from living amongst thee.

The clueless and simple, people are dumb, most of you are still children.

Mentality of infants sucking on a thumb.

I sit in silence like most my life, I watch as the abundance of people have fun.

I sit in the corner of curious and done, I sit in the dark because that's where I am from.

Alone in the world but not by my choice, for the ones I let in, they all walked away.

There are claims of love and appreciation and the claims are just that because well, where have you been?

Sure, some care and some do touch base, but mostly it's asking for my wisdom and worldly ways.

Sure, I have friends, they just aren't here; I've had some great days and relationships over the years... Wait no, they were lies; I was used, they never cared.

Where once lived a dream, the map I created lives memories of a life I've been chasing.

Where once was some hope for a circle to stay in, now is my shadow upon the walls of my dungeon.

Where once was a life that had so much to give, will one day be a stain upon the floor as a gift.

It's not lines of depression, its trials and tribulations of a misunderstood fella.

Fall of the First

Strength in numbers, brothers die, side by side.
Off in the distance, nothing but battle cries.
This is the stand, the terror of time.
These are the hands.
Mutilated and confined.

Plagues of war, forced to fight.
Nations together, unified.
Enemies turned brothers.
Fight for your rights.

Waters run red, painted fields with loss of life.
Superior weapons cut us down to defeat.
Hunted like game with no where to retreat.
Blood stained fields produce plants nothing will eat.
Broken families are left in the wake.

A prisoner off war, a slave with no name.
The language, our tongues were not to speak.
Men and women, murdered and raped.
Human trading; what price would you pay?
Millions lost, undocumented casualties.

The way of peace, destroyed in what felt like a week.
The last of us remain, cut off from society.
Lost and in pain, nothing is what it should be.
The First Nations have died.
Victims of another European genocide.

People of wisdom, people of pride.
Never had a chance but refused to hide.
Brave of the brave, at least they tried.
Plagues of war, forced to fight.
Nations together, unified.
Enemies turned brothers.
Fight for your rights.

Lost and forgotten.
Nothing left to explore.
Plagues in the blankets.
Plagues of war.
Murder in numbers, addicted to control.
Savage and reckless, will it ever end?

Do Not Comply

They want a voice of reason.
They want this perfect person.
They want a voice of reason, should be thankful this capsule remains breathing!

They paint the picture of happy.
They set the tones and watch the people chasing.
There is no room for failing.
There are no friends for the mind not playing.
Games, games, games.
Not a single fucking winner!

They want a voice of reason.
They want this perfect person.
We give all we got, we just feed the system.
They want a voice of reason, but no one's there when you are dying.

To fight for your own salvation.
Is the only fight worth something.
Free from this twisted system.
Twisted mind of the living.
Free from the restraints of another's vision.
Burning bibles, finger up.
Done with your religion.

They paint a picture of happy.
Colored bright with blood of the enemy.
Dreams of the children.
Third world visions.
They paint a picture of happy, watch all the failing.

They want a voice of reason.

They want this perfect person.

They can take all we have given, no friends for a mind fighting the system.

They want the perfect person.

Twisted mind with a twisted vision.

Take me back to the day.

The day the struggle wasn't real!

I Like Rainbows

The archive of songs is strong, sending out the messages to the disturbed and almost done.

The memories of pain left in this mind, a beehive of pain all intertwined with motives to succeed and not dwell on time.

The poetic notes piled higher than what's released because the judgement is on the fierce, song after song wrote without a note, lyrics of honest perception of visions restrained within open mind.

Knowledge of the great ones who studied all their lives, the specialists and counselors over the years gone by.

Conversation that would leave the average mind in the dirt.

List of pills taken over the years is longer than that list of betrayal you have endured.

Given the fact I know a little more then that, not here to toot this horn but that shit is a fact.

I do get messages and talk to the wind.

Fact.

Energy shifts, yeah, I get that, them eyes an open door to the soul but often times glazed over from being a shady asshole.

Not my issue though, I ain't even out trying to be in control.

Fake accounts.

Shady nights.

The voices penetrate those thin walls.

Destruction of decency is honestly just a tragedy, most of you are better and I pray that you get this letter.

Forgiveness is key to life without ongoing agony.

Forgiveness is key unless you continued to lie and lack honesty.

What's the shame in coming clean? What's them words hard to speak truly gonna do? Buried like old blood stains on the hands of thee.

Ask the question if you can handle the answer! But give the truth and end the cycle, fuckin tock tick the times wasting!

Lived life to help and try and spread joy, bent over backwards and even shared my toys.

Pitched in funds when the broke songs were sung, I fucking tied my own noose and in it I hung.

Who was there to come stand by my side? Who was there to reinstall any of my pride?

Who was there to lend that shoulder to lean on? I tell you right now, my fucking shadow was the one!

I have stories of shit that would make dead hair stand on end; I have stories with plots so thick you'd be pausing for the popcorn.

But the thing about me is: I don't give a shit no, not about that, son.

I don't get flipped or be grabbing for a clip to get some justice for all those wrongs.

I'm simply just me and I always carry on, just waiting for an honest heart to build on, waiting for some truth and some reality is all.

I'm waiting patiently like 50 in his first slim shady song.

I'm content and cruising through life, killing it one day at a time, getting wiser each hour and yet I'm compiling dark songs.

I'm happy and smiling but what I write is not right, giving the truth of where I'm from.

Delusional places in the vast background of a wide mind is all, you wouldn't understand so just group me with the depressed and move on.

Group me with the rest but I guarantee you're wrong.

Guess I'm just gifted and blessed because I lay it all to rest and peacefully step back and walk on.

No longer bowed down or out to please anyone, just conscious of purpose and doing my best to fulfill it until I'm taken..... Preferably not by my own hand....

Wtf Dot Com

What is this life, pressure and feelings?
Where is this light? This tunnel has ended.
Nothing like questions aimed at them religious opinions.
Nothing like a story wrote to entrap the people, nothing like a tale from an insightful person.

What is this Jesus and talk of disciples?
Who wrote this shit out after all those people were tortured?
Commandments upon tablets, tools to stone was the persuasion but that was so long ago and I'm not buying this delusion.
These laws make it easy to get an abortion, but suicides illegal? Now tell me that's not a type of corruption
Government made drugs but now its illegal, but them goofs up in office be hitting it harder.
Pills and crystal, smoke and coke.
Heroine in needles or powder; yeah there into the dope, making decisions in which someone's dreams are gonna shatter.

The gossip in news, the political views; what the public gets is disgusting.
I'm no longer amused.
People be talkin, flappin their jaws.
Most of em are nothing, corpse in the work force, a dick with no balls.
Say we came from China, the white people are gods; they say without Europe we'd be more than fucked.
I say its all bullshit but my ideas don't fly; after all, I'm just the awkward brown colored guy.

I ask some simple questions and get the awkward eye, but seriously why are we eating food made in a country where that exact product, you can't buy?
What about the propaganda? This world's straight fucked.

The group called the U.N is a scape goat, none the less.
Country leaders in a room trying to settle the dues, rations imposed and also them religious views.
Wars are waged and it's the turning of a page, the banks making bank, but no one even sees.
There's people dying of hunger, living in the cover of dead trees; this shit's for real, I saw them just down the street.

People are greedy about what you drive, wearing that lulu lemon and five bathroom houses up in gangster's paradise.
Wearing gold chains, them watches look like clocks, popping off at each other with gold plated gloks.
Going without food but never out of drugs, got people robbing people but they already have the same stuff.
Got bitches playing guys and acting all tough, got guys doing laundry and dishes cause their bitch is legitimately tough.
No meeting in the middle, no the line was drawn in chalk; it's been raining for years now, no one gives a fuck.

People getting depressed feeling down on their luck, razors slide through skin, also scissors and such.
Bathrooms become resting places, them weary tired faces become recycled due to impatience.
I mean yeah that knifes always waiting and the notes documented over a hundred different pages, archive of images precisely in places.
Tired souls stock piled like gold that has no actual value, it's all imaginary, sorta like most of you.
The more I venture into the source, the more I realize, and it actually almost hurts.
The more I allow the internal growth, the more I wonder if this is all a joke
I miss the days I too was just a slave, miss the days I didn't have visions of graves.
I want the times to be happy and free, I fight against the world. I battle for me.
It's hard to see the lighter side, it's kind of a crisis, I'm not gonna lie.
I sometimes feel like Isis, as I internally scream and die, explode on the inside.

Love is Dead

Love will come when you least expect it.
But they don't get the way I see it.
Love will come when you stop looking.
But you don't see the way I'm feeling.

Love will find you even if you don't see it.
But love is propaganda, riddles for children.
Friends to lovers and family alike.
Nothing is pure.
Stands the test of time.

Love will come when you love yourself.
Guess I'm done cause love is dead.
Love is an illusion like rings of marriage.
Humans are selfish and born deceivers.
Tell you they love you, sleep around and leave you.

Love is nothing when divorce is a fashion.
Money dictates who is desirable and who is worthless.
The drugs and parties, everything fancy.
Love is complicated because humans are worthless.

Pain and hatred from bad experience.
If you don't conform, they will just up and leave ya.
If you disagree, it's a silent strike against ya.
If you lose it all, who's gonna want you?
Love is dead because ego is inflated.
Decency has perished and now life is confusion.
Too bad the masses are blind to the growing devastation.
The problem is the selfish egotistical humans.

Our infatuation with the media.
Count me out.
Always been that loser.
Count me out.
I won't be part of the confusion.

Applause for the Outcast

Trapped in the moments of years long passed.
Encaged are emotions as time fades to black.
Trapped in the moments.
The dark days play back.

Engulfed in the flames.
Choking on the taste.
Who would have known the fate of those days?
Engulfed in the carnage killing off my social side.

The deafening silence is now where I reside.
The things in my head are all the conversation that's left.
Locked out, shut down, disappeared, dead.
Lost track of the days, as I miss out on years.

This life is agony for such a brilliant mind.
I am now socially awkward.
My jokes are poorly timed.
This life has left me behind.
I tried to show my love.
I tried so hard, but I couldn't speak, incomprehensible mind.

The pain of depression since I was a kid.
It has plagued and changed who I am, misunderstood.
The dark is my friend but none of you see.
I'm happiest now, when my blood runs free.
This is me now, thank you, society.

Life goes on but it's so far from free.
The price is the endless suffering.

Maybe its just me and my twisted philosophy.
But the price to pay is seldom worth the pain.
The people I loved; I now view as dead.
It's all in my head, it's all in my head.
The funny part is, I told my story, but no one believed it.

Incandescent

Startled hearts with hopes laid in grave.
Sitting in the darkness of yet another day.
Quiet songs playing in my head, not on repeat but never-ending instead.

Tired eyes, still full of sleep; wipe it away and take a stroll in moonlit streets.
Lights flicker as I'm underneath, watching them burn out incandescently.
Memories play over in my mind, they make me sad but I don't mind.

Awkwardly walking to the heartbeat, secretly wishing that I could meet.
The keeper of the stars, the one who knows who we truly are.
Though I continue on this dim lit path, I do whisper to myself.
The times are lonesome, that may be.

Though I remain in motion, progress is on the upside of oblique.
Now it's time to go to sleep, the one thing that leaves me be.
I make it home just as before, I am safe within locked doors.
I rest the spirit, the mind and soul, just to get up and repeat my stroll.
Maybe they will join me one of these days, the one who wants to stay.

Torn

Torn between the tables of probable fate.
One decision away from mistake.
One decision could terminate something great.
We all have a decision to embrace.

Torn between so many truths.
Looking at our life through the eyes of them.
Tearing the emotions out of their crate.
Unpacking the pain that made us this way.

Torn up inside, just want an escape.
To fade away, let the darkness embrace.
So many choices, swirling within.
Just empty spaces left from fair whether friends.

A look on the inside of such a palace of glass.
One stone toss away from the greatest collapse.
Torn between the memories of the past.
Dissection revealed the patterns; tests we didn't pass.

So, we write it all out like a broken record.
Write day and night, hoping to feel better.
Write passages and songs of defeat.
Wrote maybe twice of love and positive belief.
But in the end, it was just a tale, self defeat.

Torn between the tables of probable fate.
Torn between the next choice we will make.
Torn inside as we renounce our faith.
Torn open wide, torn with limited pride.

Between Thin Lines

Twisted tails of life with strange skills, leaving pages turning as books are dropped into the flaming kilns.

Lifeless without a pardon for those forgotten, outcasts raked over the coals.

Schools ended but the torture and resentment left from a past of leaking tears.

Emotions were so high, left nerves permanently fried with thoughts locked inside drowning in the rip tide, nothing new in obscure.

People ask why I feel dead inside but I give no honest reply because I've been open for years.

Talk all the time; I shared my secrets inside and only got the answers, advice I already tried.

I'm a failure, this is clear.

There's a different meaning in that so just relax, you obviously don't have a clue.

I've got a lot of pride; I just hide it deep inside with the cadavers of slain prejudice and fear.

Overcome every obstacle and truly did it on my own, well I suppose I had my soul.

We became the best of friends.

18 years inside, fighting for my life though I know I'm not alone.

There may be one or two in whom I confide but lately that seems like it was pretend.

Kinda wonder where they went until I realize that I left without intent; I'm kinda in the way of my own life.

Who would've thought I'd spend all these years in my self created box without Pandora in sight.

Never would have guessed I'd be my biggest test as I'm clearly blind to who actually cares.

I married my demon; she did not win but actually excelled me at life.

Chased down my dreams and became captain of my team as I surpass my own predicted life.

I can't help but try even when I feel my time would be better applied if I would unsubscribe to my outlook on life and become blind.

But how can I retire from this life when I've experienced so much, seriously searching for answers but nothing catches my eye.

Sentenced to this lifeline, I'll push through, its all fine.

Sentenced in my mind doesn't deserve its own line, I'll push through, I will be fine.

Ya just don't mind, I'll be fine

Just waiting, passing time but I'll be fine, I swear.

Bitch

I left it on the line.
I offered a passage to my heart.
I granted a pathway to bypass a lot of shit.
I left it on the line.
The feelings on my sleeve.
I granted a moment, opening unto my abyss.

I feel it slowly burning.
Feel the flesh boil, watch the blister formulate.
I smell the cauterization.
The scab peels and festers away.
I feel the death of tomorrow.
Do not resuscitate.
I see the darkness coming.
It steals my breathe and fills me with hate.

I left my cage open.
My life flame, free to take.
Heart upon my sleeve.
I tried to articulate.
All of my emotions, nothing's what it seems.
I left my cage open and watched you walk away.

I got up every morning.
Mourning all my pain.
I got up every morning.
I walked through all the rain.
I push through every moment.
Numb from all my pain.
I woke up screaming, calling out your name.

Calling out your name.
Screaming out in vain.
Regrets of yesterday, haunting memories.

I feel it slowly burning.
Feel the flesh boil, watch the blister formulate.
I smell the cauterization.
The scab peels and festers away.
I feel the death of tomorrow.
Do not resuscitate.
I see the darkness coming.
It steals my breath and fills me with hate.

I cut my rib cage open.
My heart upon your plate.
Never tasted it, you fucking threw it away.
I left myself open.
I bottled all my pain.
I just want to feel love.
To be needed by another again.
I need to stop this cycle.
I need to be free from all this rage.

I can't remember why I cut myself that day.
I left a fucking trail, crimson memory.
You fed me that medication.
You poisoned my fucking brain.
Ambulance came faster than I had ever seen.
Trapped for two weeks.
That institution now plagues my fucking dreams.

I feel it slowly burning.
Feel the flesh boil and watch the blister formulate.
I smell the cauterization.
The scab peels and festers away.
I feel the death of tomorrow.
Do not resuscitate.
I see the darkness coming.
It steals my breath and fills me with hate.

I spent fucking years.
I wasted all my days.
I combed every moment.
Looking for something to explain.
We had the best thing going.
We had a life made up of all our dreams.
Why so much lying? Why so much hate?
You came home from work and wouldn't look into my eyes.

Gladly take all my money.
Let me pay for your life.
Ditch me for another plan, one you never made.
Left me out, alone.
I fought three people that night.
I still don't have a friend, a person who is by my side.
You slept on the couch, as I lay awake at night.
Follow you out the doors to see you climb into his ride.
Followed you through hell.
And they wonder why I'm so dry.

I feel it slowly burning.
Feel the flesh boil and watch the blister formulate.
I smell the cauterization.
The scab peels and festers away.
I feel the death of tomorrow.
Do not resuscitate.
I see the darkness coming.
It steals my breath and fills me with hate.
I feel it all drowning.
I no longer feel pain.
I am in love with another.
But they don't feel the same.
So, I sit and ponder.
If it's all the same.
I can't help but wonder.
Is life gonna rape me everyday?

Violet

Catch the sky through violet eyes.
Bask in the essence of living without the crutch of fears, no tears just clear eyes.
Grab the moment, don't let it pass by.
Deep breathe for a moment and pursue life with limits set sky high.

Live life without boundaries, set yourself free.
Don't think too much on what could be.
Life is a gift, self created catastrophe.
Buckle at the knees from such monotony.
Clawing at the surface, screaming like a banshee.

Stop looking for a reason
Stop asking to be free.
Not given a direction
No map to the path at our feet.

Life lived within a passion for the new sun to rise.
Living within freedom of our own minds.
Be one with the echo that taunts as you lay down for sleep.
Embrace the intrigue, pursue cautiously.
Live life in the moment and be happy please.
Live with a smile, for the ones trapped in sorrow webs, fallen on bruised knees.

It's ok to be depressed but let the moment pass.
It's ok because I know what its like to live repressed.
Living with knots in the neck, walking with thoughts in the dirt.

Stop looking for a reason
Stop asking to be free.
Not given a direction.

No map to the path at our feet.
Stop to smell the flowers.
Stop wasting precious time.
Take back your power and step into the light.

Bring Back the Light

As I lay dying in the dark;
I find my place, a calling for another start.
As I lay withering in full decay.
I arise from the casket of yesterday.

Black magic's hex from a tortured soul.
These chains I will break.
I will regain control.
Black magic curses that pin me down.
I break the hold and send it back around.

Give me peace; I can't take much more.
Grant release from this darkness I know as home.
Give me faith, a day with honest light.
Give me strength as I claw my way back to life.

As I lay dying with no remorse.
As I lay here fractured, broke.
This pine wood box is not a home.
This place in the dirt, I was left to drown.
This malice wished by a jealous soul.
I break this hex, I regain control.

As I lay dying under haunted skies.
Within my element, in the night.
Under Orion's belt, I cast out the energy.
A reversal from this witch's heart.
As I lay dying under starlit skies.
I break your grasp and block my mind.

Now, to watch the night cascade to light.
With the powers through me, I return your blight.
The hex, the curse and lack of life.
I amplify it and drain your life.
Inflicted pain and all the curse.
Back to the sender, times six.

Light Summary from Depressive Slavery

Darkness indeed, thoughts woven with black, making it difficult to breathe. Sludge courses, as this blackened heart forces the fluids to sustain life; truth is, it's death that is running from me. Demons hold grudges and the sisters of fate remain judgeless because they hold fear. Apart in the mind, I'm not alone up in here. The voices, they talk, and the actions take part when the dark gates part. My thoughts are to be feared. No longer a spark, no sanity is part of the path I walk and I no longer fucking care.

Darkness indeed, it's time that I let myself become free, to let the shit out that I choke down unpleasantly, indefinitely.

The words I left unspoken because I'm the bigger version of the lower me. Internally battle the words that so desperately seek to leak from inside of me. The visions I place in the cages behind fiery gates, locked so deep down inside of the dark mess, darkness of the tainted mentality.

Think the demons are who come to me; seek the knowledge of my self mastery. Savagery is great indeed; I'm not all about rainbows and crystal-clear creeks. Where's the blood roses woven into nooses, please. I'm nice by the choice, not the fear of what lies beneath. I'm haunted with images that would drop a true human to their fucking knees. Aware of the attacks and the half witted entities.

Darkness of a mind plagued over more years than you would care, than you would allow yourself to consume this crisp, stale air. The nightmares of life that I lived with while I was awake made sleep the closest thing to glee for me.

The rivers run red with all the blood shed when the inner dark comes out to play, the desires of scandalous endeavors created from something behind the line. The thought of time being measured in a millisecond is baffling when the moment is never ending but, forever unforgiven and is the creation of this madness in which I'm driven.

Spell on me, to use my own demon to conquer the will I have to keep the blood within this vessel, forever coursing. I thank you, dearly, for failing to get to me; I love my darkness, it brings me my kindness because my mind's been forever a mess. Hit me with madness, I'll write and get closer to famous because I'm relentless with a past that nothing matches.

Nothing sent, nor nothing said will have an actual effect. I send that shit back times three, times three. I'm higher than the witch and bitch, better believe I'm gonna live more than free. Sick and twisted in the mindset, knowing I can end this is my power over that lower vibration that was me.
I circle myself in full pentagram and seal it in vivid light, violet laced with white for all eternity. North, east, south, west; I call upon the universal memory. I command that you acknowledge my pure, true identity. To the spirits and the world beyond what the naked eye can see, I ask that you hear me and reverse the crippling energy intended for ending me.

Darkness indeed, is strong in me but with darkness is light and that's what I use for the better of reality. With darkness is wisdom, passed over from multiple lives and each individual fantasy. Darkness I bring, in my modest and powerful peace. And with darkness, I see, oh so vividly.

The Cleansing (Song)

Rose lay upon the stone, blood red with blood stained thorns.
Tragic loss of this life, no sorrows here through the dusk of night.
Skies paved black with not a chance of hope, my back remains forever broke.

Roses lay down at thy feet, honestly, just another eulogy.
Friend of yesterday rots in the mind, because this being has long served their time.
People come and people go, but its people who bring such lack of hope.
Wish we may and wish we might, ending is always dismay and its time to turn out the light.

Precision placed blade at the throat, pull it clean and in slow-mo.
Ropes tied tight from head to toe because escaping this torture has no hope.
No gag, let's hear them screams, watch the endless suffering.
Now it's your chance to beg and plead, ask me why as you tremble and bleed.

Rose laid upon the stone, blood red with blood stained thorns.
Tragic loss of this life, no sorrows here through the dusk of night.
Skies paved black with not a chance of hope, my back remains forever broke.

Paint the picture, the tests of life.
Choosing victims based on strife.
Take it further than prepared; make them remember who is to be feared.
The blood cleans easy with bleach and mop; the bodies collect in the corner to rot.
Smell reminds of grim success for another victim has been crossed off this list.

How many more will have to bow at there knees.
Become dismembered bloodless remains.
Just fill for the hole known as a grave.
Who's the evil and who's the victim, just killing off the superstition?
Bodies of demons, my old friends.
These massacres are priceless, celebration of sirens songs.

Rose laid upon the stone, blood red with blood stained thorns.
Tragic loss of this life, no sorrows here through the dusk of night.
Skies paved black with not a chance of hope, my back remains forever broke.

So, lay these roses and remember those pleas, I'll forever smile in bloody glee.
Limbs of bodies mixed and matched, these remains will never be brought back.
Satan's army at these feet, the sacrifice is so bittersweet.
People come and people go, but all these chosen never had hope.

Rose laid upon the stone, blood red with blood stained thorns.
Tragic loss of this life, no sorrows here through the dusk of night.
Skies paved black with not a chance of hope, my back remains forever broke.

The Weight That Kills Me

Stuck inside myself again.
Violent awakening pinned for the suffering.
Stuck in between the realms.
Between myself again.
Paralysis slowly setting in, struggle but show no signs of fight.
Choking, as the demon takes his grip.
The motherfucker they call life!

Stuck inside myself again.
Days painted black, stuck in my old ways can't win.
Can't help myself when only they see a problem.
Losing my mind, trying to conform to you.
Losing myself just to belong somewhere.
Fuck it, I'm out; this struggle is too far from real.

So, I want but will never say.
Never gonna let myself portray, never gonna want you.
In myself, I see; I justify my pain.
I know I am me, what I've been through.
Never gonna be you, not gonna happen.
Take your image of man and leave, my world doesn't have room for you.

Stuck in myself again, stuck fighting pretend.
Sometimes I let it win, let the darkness consume me.
All these people with multiple faces.
It's a hard life when no body wants to be real.
It's like there is no purpose in life when nobody else can see it.
Dumbstruck, a society living from ego.

Stuck in myself again, bet you think its suffering.
Not living my best life.
No good times.
Stuck in the veil again, having a heart to heart with a demon.
Social media is the new sworn-in religion.
The tool used to brainwash the nations.
But it's ok, I know it's suffer or get out.

I awake, pinned down, paralyzed again.
I'd fight it but there isn't a fuck left in me.
Pinned and choking me, slowly I wake up.
The recipe to start the day, I know it's coming for me.
But I know it's suffer or get out.
So, believe in me when I freely say.
I'd rather take my own life.
I'd rather suffer alone and hide it.
Than abandon my spirit and change my ways.

I love you but, I love me, and I know you judge me.
In the loneliness, in me.
It is comforting.
Knowing absolutely nothing.
Aware, but not saying.
Maybe you do want me, but I'm too disrupted to notice.
That's just me, I'm just existing in anguish.
It's not you, it's the voices that are screaming.
I'm here, but my time is coming.

Stitches torn, no fixing.
Nothing to mend, I'm not living in pretend.
There's no way; I say fuck that!
I mean, all I say, all the feelings were muted.
You mean the world, my friend.
I'd stand by you till the end.
But I'm nervous to say it.

Stuck in my head again, stuck in my pretend.
Trying to figure my way out.
Crossed the veil again and this time, it feels like I'm trapped in the cloud.
The black of my mindset.
I'd fight it again, but it never lets up.
It never lets up!

At Peace

The hands of time, turning so slow, the days roll by as the story unfolds.
Awake and sleep based on sunsets, living in peace, learning to lose regrets.
Sun goes down and that moon comes up, dull light shines beautifully in the darkened sky.
Day by day, night by night.
Admire it all with the mind opened wide.

These hands of time move so slow, would swear that this clock is broke.
Decisions made with lack of thought, decisions persuade what's to come on our clock.
Time moves on, never in reverse, but this time around its movement is almost cursed.
Night by night, reflecting on the day, wandering that alternate reality.
The should have and should nots of moments long passed. Admire the story and convert the sorrow to laughs.

It's all for a reason, it's like a retest, it's just oh so boring without a self created mess.
These hands on the clock, old father time.
He's got it figured out if we could just choose right.
Clocks fall to pieces, they decay on the wall.
It's like the clocks are broken, they are moving so slow.
If I could change those hands of kept time, perhaps I would be ahead of life right here, right now.
If I could go back in hypothetical thought, I bet a lot wouldn't know me or maybe asleep under the cross.

The hands of time are moving so slow; I think it's time to rethink and grow.
But right now, on this day, my self worth and love has hit home.
For as of today, the regrets, I let go. It's time to say bye to the past; it's time to cut cords and start over fresh.
It's time to be thankful for the opportunity to have a retest.
Today I am grateful, I don't feel blue.
And today, I look forward to tomorrow and to do something new.

Patience Consumes

Home at last, in the loneliness I bask, waiting for my cue.

Sit and wait, play no games, just in company with these thoughts and some memories in review.

Thoughts of the times I wasn't confined, suffocating under such twisted rule.

Thoughts cross the line and it's time to remind myself of all I've lived through.

At home and alone, an imagination out of control, jumping from view to view.

The silence is gone; it's been way too long, I don't even know what I'd do.

How would I cope without the torment from my ghost? This question isn't new.

I wouldn't last, based on my past, if the silence was to come through.

It's too much to ask and my psyche would collapse, as I'm rushed off to that padded room.

Alone in my mind, at home or outside, the emptiness is where I'm doomed.

I can always relate and help chase the fog away but that's only for others, it's true.

I talk to myself and ask out for help, but it's just an echo in a vacant room.

I forgive that I'm forgotten and that's where it's at; this life has shown me more than it has you.

I could be humble and not cause any trouble, but that's just not gonna do.

So, I sit, and I wait; I count all these days and I hold memories while others fade because I choose me before you.

I see way too much, and I hate when you bluff, thinking I don't have a clue.

I shut down and disappear; it's easier than lending an ear and hearing another bullshit story.

So, I still sit, and I wait, and I ask everyday, but no one is listening.

Feel breath fade away as I start to suffocate, choking on words never spoken.

But hey, it's ok; after all, it's only me: the one who gives even when broken.

It's only me, the one who is so carefree; never talks of the pain he is holding.

Just this guy, a man alone in the crowd, built of all the things in which you are looking.

So, I sit, and I wait, and I listen attentively as the story keeps unfolding.

As I sit, quietly choking.

Still Waiting

Show me an angel, I'll show you a demon.
It's truly a choice to see only the good in people.
It's bullshit to be judged against the vacant pedestal.
Held to a standard no one's achieving.
God is an idea, not a documented being!

Do as your told, not as we do.
Read this book, it knows all.
Read the stories to teach you how to be living.
Read this gift, this book of fables.
Ideas compiled to feed a purpose, to guide the sheep into organizations.
Lies are the foundation of all we believe in.

You know what? Fuck it, God! Give me a reason!
I'll sit, I'll wait, watch the turn of all the seasons.
As days go by without your presence.
The part where you don't exist, becomes more apparent.
But wait, that can't be; it doesn't seem right.
Let me take a moment to re read this bullshit.
Oh here, in the fine print.
We are God, he fucking resides inside us.
Here, they are preying like children.
Worship the clouds and ignore what's in them.

Pass the collection plate over here!
I don't need to feed the children.
Pay out cash with a smile.
That money isn't taxed, the pastor is Gucci.
Support the cause, the ones who cleansed nations.
The ones who pillaged and raped.

Burning women and children.
To the pyres and the iron maiden.
The law set by breaking all the humans.

Count me out, I don't fall for your corruption.
I won't stand to be apart of something that rapes the children.
I won't bow my head to please you people.
I'll just do me and be more enlightened.
I believe I'm something called my personal opinion.
Here's some advice, a new direction.
Praise yourself on being a better person.
Save your money and invest in tomorrow.
Accept your fate and try not to live in the sorrow.
Life is shit, a pointless endeavor.
If you meet another who makes you see and feel.
Who opens your mind to infinite delusions.
Keep 'em around and ignore the part where we're dying.

Just Be True

Darkness is the product of light, darkness balances all in life.
Darkness is attached at the feet, grateful this darkness never leaves.
Black is the truth, the shadow living with us all.

What test is harder? To stand again or was it to fall?
To love again? Or collecting the remains of your heart off the floor?
The broken has the story and the author is not to be found.
For truth is kind of tricky, the other half is never heard, like the shadow upon the ground.

Actions are reflections, pages from our tales, slipping out with every sound.
These actions say more than the voice will ever tell.
And sometimes these actions come from that same shadow that lives in us all.

Patience is a gift, though sometimes feels like a curse.
Interference with others lives because of jealousy, envy or pride.
The storm can be waited out as the suffering subsides.
Maybe life wouldn't be so hard if you didn't fabricate such intricate lies?
Maybe try living with balance of the darkness and the light.
Judgment placed is an emotional waste, adding to the baggage of personal disgrace.

Vultures waiting for their cue, picking each other apart is nothing new.
What is a friend, is it just a point of view?
What is a lie if being honest is nothing to you.
What is life, the greatest waste of time.
Nothing even matters as the life fades into the sand.

Like black cast from light, tortured spirits live on.
Add to the suffering if you think you can, add to your self as karma carries on.
Glad that honest is at least far and few.
Appreciate that it's not forever gone and can be renewed.

To What do I Owe

To what do I owe.
The price of living selfless.
Left me to die alone.
The disease progresses.
Time erodes.

Oh, the tales I know.
New days, brightly lit.
Casting the darkest shadow.
My place, my home.
To what do I owe, what do I owe.

Time moves on and I'm dying so.
Nobody knows, nobody's home.
Try to win but the disease took control.
The thanks I get for having hope.
The friends I have that never think to say hello.

Oh, to what do I owe, what did I know.
My frustration in these last days.
Being helpful while losing hope.
Don't bother with a service.
You let me battle this alone.
Rest in peace, that hits home.

Remember me not.
For you never remembered me at all.
I reach out, but nobody is home.
I set the intent and I was ignored.
I fought this tiring fight.

But the disease won, after all.
I have a number of days.
Nobody to call.
To what do I owe, no explanation and even less hope.
Selfless being that was thrown out.
To no one I owe, I'm living my fear as I am dying alone.

Appreciate the Music

The songs sang, saving people from pain.
Reminding ourselves we are not the insane.
The journey of a lifetime accompanied without a lifeline.
Tales of the hard times to love and walks in the moonlight.
Stories of criminal to lessons of the unpredictable.

Artists, these idols singing out for all of us.
The torture and torment, the feeling of giving up.
The life and the laughter, uplifting us as we continue to battle.

In the moments of weakness, climbing over walls and obstacles just to save us.
What is fear if you face it, commonly said in the playlist.
Words formed from the intuitive, seducing like a sedative.

Tough times are relentless, nights become restless.
Searching within for some sort of answers, craving forgiveness.
The body and mind weaken from the stress, life starts to feel oh so relentless.
Then you get that reminder, you here some lyrics that pick up your spirits.

Just for a moment the mess becomes painless, and in that moment we receive a reset.
Music is timeless when the words vibe with us.
Its healing power is from an understanding, it's just a shame when it's the artist that needs the saving.

Artists, these idols singing out for all of us.
The torture and torment, the feeling of giving up.
The life and the laughter, uplifting us as we continue to battle.

Sing for the moment, sing for the pleasure.
Remember all the lyrics feel the power.
Appreciate all those who have fallen.
As well as the ones who still remain breathing.

The tales of torment, the heartache and success.
Fables of events, places and relatable topics.
Words can be weapons, razor blades piercing delicate flesh.
Suicide and murder, lost souls leaving behind useless flesh.
Ghostly encounters that depict a sense of emotionless.

There's reason for all of this, the message is between twisted lines.
Behind empty promises.
Relatable subjects and emotions of the populous.
Taken from deep inside the minds of the greatest.
Lines spoken for the ones who just feel speechless.

Closed Eyes

Do you know, can you find?
Can you tolerate what isn't felt inside?
Can you see the jagged walls?
Do you hear the warning bells, chiming as another takes their life?

Do you get the world inside?
Or are you running to save your life?
Pulled out by the tide, left alone to drown and die.
To drown and die!

Is it all that we can do, is there any hope to renew?
Is it all we can see? Take it all.
All away from me, holding memories deep inside.
Fighting demons late at night.
Wondering again, how did we get here?
Tell me how we got here!

As the battles come through closed doors.
Emotions to blame for waging war.
Seems the anticipation of the death bed's all we have left.
Seeing people smiling.
Wonder if it's real, please.
Tell me I'm dreaming.
I'm dreaming!

Do you get the world inside?
Or are you running to save your life?
Pulled out by the tide, left alone to drown and die.
To drown and die!

I think this ship is sinking!
It's time to leave it.
Abandon hope, run and hide.
Abandonment to save our lives.
Let it burn, tell me why.
Why should we fight back?
Fight back!

All these people by your side.
None of them see your desperate cries.
Depression runs its course, turning joy into remorse.
Remorse for taking every breathe.
The dying urge to not wake up.
The taunting voice inside the head.
Screaming out to end it.
To end it.

Do you get the world inside?
Or are you running to save your life?
Pulled out by the tide, left alone to drown and die.
To drown and die!

Out on the gallows we finally see.
All that could have been.
Living hallow, broken bones.
The stories there, in the undertones.
Burning bridges, nothing new.
No words left, too much abuse.

Parting out inside your head.
Painting pictures of the alternate.
What if it could be?
What if it would be?
Not calling out for help, no one gets the things felt.
Not giving that chance, someone cared enough to ask.
I think it's hard for people to see.
How they smile while suffering.

Do you get the world inside?
Or are you running to save your life?
Pulled out by the tide, left alone to drown and die.
To drown and die!

I think this ship is sinking!
It's time to leave it.
Abandon hope, run and hide.
Abandonment to save our lives.
Let it burn, tell me why.
Why should we fight back?
Fight back!

Loops

Silence sweeps through the broken streets.
The home inside the mind.
Left in dismay, disbelief of what has come of today.
Wondering, lost in confusion as thoughts project our worst fears.
Evil comes to life, a new companion.

Silence: it creeps, penetrates and infects, speeding up time inside.
All that's left is to become counterfeit, just a shell of a man, human.
With every step, trying to escape it.
That clutch of the monster within.

So lie down amongst the beast, offer yourself and give up one more piece.
One part of the puzzle, one more memory fades to black.
Knowing damn well there's no point in striking back.
Consumed with the heat, becoming another devils advocate.
Keep it discreet, ya just another filthy secret.

Just go away, leave. It's not like anyone can see it.
Gonna be awhile before time brings some forgiveness.
Watching you stand by, gone but never forgotten.
Perhaps you could save a soul tattered and torn?
Perhaps you are the secret to killing these demons?
But you aren't here, just in imagination.

Petals of the heart, slowly they wither.
The glass inside the mind, fractured, stressed but not broken.
The distance in time, space and emotion.
The punishment is unfit for the crime never committed.
Forever singled out to pay for another.
Alone, in the storm, in life it's a given.

Live the double life that you were forced to create within.
We're all dying to live, happy or not, it's part of the system.
Bottle it up, speak of it not, force a smile.
Purposely reversing, dissociative.
Give them what they want, give in to self neglect.
Pressure from the masses to be top of the classes.
Have to be happy or face abandonment.

The mass of the world becomes harder to hold.
Back starts breaking, gotta ignore it or they will be done with you.
Everyone wants to help but no one is able to care.
The words often leave their lips but where the fuck do they go?
Looks like it's on loop as the events don't feel new.

That's when..
Silence, it creeps, penetrates and infects, speeding up time inside.
All that's left is to become counterfeit, just a shell of a man, human.
With every step, trying to escape it.
That clutch of the monster within.

Her we stand alone as one, connected, one thing in common.
The battle, it continues.
The war wages on.
Last moment looking up, hoping to lay eyes upon a better view.
The place in the dirt, the black, it feels like home.
Hate how good it sounds, impending doom.
Just when nothing's left, another breeze filters through.
The haze dissipates and the silence breaks through.

So lie down amongst the beast, offer yourself and give up one more piece.
One part of the puzzle, one more memory fades to black.
Knowing damn well there's no point in striking back.
Consumed with the heat, becoming another devils advocate.
Keep it discreet, ya just another filthy secret.

Just go away, leave, its not like anyone can see it.
Gonna be a while before time brings some forgiveness.
Watching you stand by, gone but never forgotten.
Perhaps you could save a soul tattered and torn?
Perhaps you are the secret to killing these demons?
But you aren't here, just in imagination.

Petals of the heart, slowly they wither.
The glass inside the mind fractured, stressed but not broken.
The distance in time, space and emotion.
The punishment is unfit for the crime never committed.
Forever singled out to pay for another.
Alone, in the storm, in life its a given.

Live the double life that you were forced to create within.
We're all dying to live, happy or not, its part of the system.
Bottle it up, speak of it not, force a smile.
Purposely reversing, dissociative.
Give them what they want, give in to self neglect.
Pressure from the masses to be top of the classes.
Have to be happy or face abandonment.

The mass of the world becomes harder to hold.
Back starts breaking, gotta ignore it or they will be done with you.
Everyone wants to help but no one is able to care.
The words often leave them lips but where the fuck do they go?
Looks like its on loop, same old, same old.

That's when..
Silence, it creeps, penetrates and infects, speeding up time inside.
All that's left is to become counterfeit, just a shell of a man, human.
With every step, trying to escape it.
That clutch of the monster within.

Here we stand alone as one, connected, one thing in common.
The battle, it continues.
The war wages on.
Last moment looking up, hoping to lay eyes upon a better view.
The place in the dirt, the black, it feels like home.
Hate how good it sounds, impending doom.
Just when nothings left, another breeze filters through.
The haze dissipates and the silence breaks through.

This cycle is real but isn't new.

The Dream

Could you believe in an alternate reality?
The mirror images of our lives, only the roles have been reversed.
Could you believe? close your eyes, tell me you can't see.
To live in the world where the pain goes away.
To experience all the joy, blissful, carefree.

Could you believe in a better life?
Living in a loving, peaceful society.
Could you believe, faith in the world, living free from deceit.
Close your eyes and you can see, the best version of ourselves, finally set free.

Could you believe in an alternate reality?
Can you see life in a world so free?
Life with peace, a life for you and me.
Standing together, connected in harmony.

Dream away, dream away.
Dream it all away.
Dream away, dream away
Dream it all away

Away with the violence, away from us.
Away with the silence, slowly killing us.
Away with the hatred, we can't take no more.
Away with the government, forcing lies down our throat.

Take the torture of lives long past.
Die with honor, not with knives in our backs.
Stand together, stand with pride.
Stand together, completely unified.
Take the torture of lives long past, no more silence, you can have that back.

Could you believe in an alternate reality?
Could you believe in being free?
Could you believe? tell me you can see.
A world healthy below our feet, a world wealthy with equality.
Another dimension that looks like this, but one thing's different.
It's built on love and innocence.

Could you believe in an alternate reality?
Can you see life in a world so free?
Life with peace, a life for you and me.
Standing together connected in harmony.

Dream away, dream away.
Dream it all away.
Dream away, dream away
Dream it all away

No more depression, no more disease.
No more oppression, just get what you see.
Lose all the lying, the cheating and deceit.
Lose all the violence, no room for all the webs that it weaves.

Breaking the habit as the dark falls away.
Like waves on the beach, cleansing all eternity.
Smiles upon every face we see.
Happy and content, living purposefully.
No need for drugs and substance, too much abuse.
Nothing but clear minds, living in a euphoria, enjoying the views.

That thing called heaven, that dream deep within.
Instead of the hell on earth that a lot live within.
Some won't get it, some can't see the strain.
Some are lucky and aren't subject to being drained.
The darkness and poor thoughts that plague such innocent minds
Feeling the other people's pain, knowing too much, getting whispers from the
wind.

Close your eyes, just pretend.
See the euphoria, let it sink in.

Our Timeline

Time is life and life is time.
Think about it for a second, let it consume the mind.
Seconds to minutes and hours to days.
Days fade away.
All that's left is the memories retained.

Everything is measured, it's not a debate.
Self worth doesn't wager in on the money you make.
Million-dollar man with the heart of pure gold.
Making just enough to dream, but not to afford.

Born into the world with no place to go.
Given a set date for demise engraved in the genetic code.
We wait for a better tomorrow and struggle through today.
Spend most our lives at work, dreaming about play.
Days turn too weeks and months fade away.

Another birthday dies in the ashes of yesterday.
You can't plan your life based on the clock.
Better act now before motivation is lost.
Life is too short is the tail often told.
It's kinda hard to live it when living takes all of your gold.

This currency, this issue, the common of man.
The wealth or lack of, depending on individual ambition.
This time to do, in the time frame of the unknown.
Man created the day, that measurement we all know.
Groups of numbers and names that this whole world knows.

Essentially it works, organizes the chaos, and synchronizes the show.
Though we each expire at our own rate.

It's our own fate; though we can estimate it I'm sure.
So why wait for the next twenty-four?
What if it's the end in an hour or so?
Don't wait, it tempts fate, live for you.
The jobs we obtain based on our comfort or wage.
None of it matters if you're miserable at the end of the day.

Seen some homeless smiling honestly, that should tell you a couple of things.
I guess it's just the life we wish to uphold.
You need to have enough to get by, to eat and stay warm on them cold winter nights.
To make the payments on the way, you get to your job, the place you spend most of your life.
To supply your own stuff just to do your job, another expense on the list.
You need to have enough to enjoy the things that you love.
To avoid deep depression and all that fun stuff, you need to deal with bullshit.

So you need to find out what your good at.
Something you enjoy is a must, I may add.
Then you need to dumb yourself down and be a good little sheep.
Do as you're told by someone who can't, the normal of society.
You need to be ok with ridicule and being second guessed.
Doubted, disbelief can be the source of harsh stress.
To explain yourself a million times in one day.
Just to come back the next and do it all again.
After so many years of working this loop, you'll start to form very different views.

Ask yourself if this is actually you?
No longer feel authentic, lost touch with the inner truth.
Forcing out a smile or drinking the stress away.
Walking around in denial, enraged that life turned out this way.
Maybe then you will see, it's not how much you have, it's you did with each and everyday.
Make it count before life fades to grey.

*wrote this a while ago, figured I'd finally share.
For those who check in and stuck by my side, much love.
For those who never have time to say hi, I understand.
For those of you who can relate, I'm here to talk anytime any day.*

Prescription for Life

Standing on the roof top, shouting out at the sky.
Echo in the darkness resembles the hole deep inside.
Scream for the answers.
Scream for forgiveness.
Most of all, scream for a reason why.

Standing on the rooftop but collapse from the pain under the sky.
Standing everyday with no one, only memory is suffering with no reason inside.
Living in loneliness is the only option and I don't know why.
Live in the moment.
Ignore the hopeless, the resentment towards life.

Try and forget it.
Focus on living, for tomorrow is a new day.
Can't escape it, wanting to end it without causing family pain.
Why is it selfish to cease existence, draining red substance of life?
How is it helping to continue breathing when there's nothing left of your light?
How is it worth the struggle when you're dead on the inside?
No wrong or right.

Standing on the rooftop, screaming out at the night.
Standing in the blackness, that color that is the mind.
Could just end this; open the wrists up nice and wide.
Thin the blood out with a bottle, drowning inside.
Celebrating alone again for the last time.
There's nowhere left to hide and no room for goodbye.

Threats of hell sound appealing when you can't find a purpose in life.
The stories consume as we reach and turn out the last light.
Drown in the open, drown in the ocean.

The shit that we are told isn't right.
At last no more gasping, struggling to see.
No more panic, nothing left.
Lost all dignity.

Can't stand the liars and users, the deceit and the guilt.
Can't take the memories of all the times I was intentionally hurt.
The bullies, the teachers that made me feel like shit.
The lectures, the violence, being kicked to the dirt.
The lovers turn to demons as they purposely tear us apart.

Abandoned by the system because the pills never fixed.
High on prescriptions, looking for a place I would fit.
Therapists and counselors, always repeating the same shit.
That loner, that outcast, so sick of it.
The daydreams, the dark themes that run wild through the head.

The questions that plague since it all started.
The answer is that we never wanted this.
That feeling of sorrow, the hopelessness.
The tears and the torment, choking with every breath.
It's the knowing that life has never given a reason to feel like this.
Nothing to blame for being consumed in darkness.
Wanting to feel like all the rest, wanting release from the thoughts we suppress.
Swallow more pills and let the numbing of our souls be the reason we exist.
No one will ever understand how it feels to be condemned in hopelessness.
To live on prescriptions, suffering from side affects too embarrassing to discuss.

People voicing the opinion that we bring it on ourselves.
The rumors and discrimination based on intolerance.
For too many years, putting up with all of this.
No longer fear of leaving into the abyss.
Exit life with two well placed slits.
Leaving tonight, giving up on life, calling it quits.

Thoughts 1

Woke up from a dream, dazed, sitting on the cold ground.
Dark, the light faded in.
Confused again, is this the best part of tomorrows yesterday?
Finding my shadow, bury its face into palm.

Woke from the blurred vision, how long was I standing there?
What happened, where did I go?
Why the confusion, seriously what the fuck am I doing here?
Look at the time but I can't see, are these hands even moving?
Do I even care?

Woke up from deaths grip one more time, dreams fade as I begin to remain.
Life in motion, everyday feels the same.
In the state of dream, I find my happiness it seems, drifting away losing touch,
escaping reality.

Dreams of finding a place.
Visions of friends.
Dreams of my favorite place.
I can smell the two stroke fumes.

Dreaming is how I escape.
Memories of the people I hold dear.
Hugs on snow covered peaks.
Learning how to overcome some of my fear.
The riding in B.C, family time in my youth.
Winter means the most to me, its clear.

I wake again, staring into the abyss in the dim lit hall, look at the time again.
Still cant read the clock upon the wall.

All this time is gone and it hits so hard.
I'm not a kid anymore and what have I got to show?
I dream of acceptance, of finding a place to belong.
To share my life experience, to not die alone.

It must be a dream though, it's been so long.
Materialistic is the world right now.
Adventure means sacrifice, something I truly know, but do you?
The best moments have been from leaving the comfort of a warm home.
What happened to the world, what the hell went wrong?

So I drift off into a dream again, in my mind is where I belong.
In the moment with friends, I imagine it all.
No more silent tears, as I do it all alone.
No more honest fear of dying out there on my own.
In my mind I am loved, in my mind I feel in touch.
Not so guarded, don't have to be tough.
In my dream, I'm appreciated.
The one place I get to be loved.
In myself I constantly have confided, it's all I've known.
All that's left.

Some say it's a choice, that I am a victim of myself.
Some say I'm hard to accept, my indifference with how people choose to live their life.
I'm hard to be around, too serious, unable to laugh.
Humour is too dry, make it awkward.
Never smile.

I admit it, I'm different, truly though.
Front to back, in fact I am honestly surprised.
My psyche is intact, that it even exists.
I'm truly amazed, look at me, still here.
Living off the mind numbing pills.
Not medicated, but is my mind even clear?

I wasn't always so fucked up; my mind wasn't always an organized mess.
My story, that shits a hard one because it's been off limits.
Untold stories, personal experience that created this.

The person I am today, constantly drifting off in a daydream.
The person you see, that person is only a reflection of the reality.
Could probably write a novel, another group of words nobody reads.
Put it next to the dictionary and the thesaurus too.

I act like I don't care, ya it's true.
It's not a lie, I can't afford to.
I act like myself, do you?
I get lost in my dream world and it's still more real than a lot of you.
Walking depictions of what you think you should be.
Walking shadows, sheep of society.
I'm fading out, need a break.
Could mean a thing or two...

Black Hearts Bleed Red

Can you feel the block within your throat?
Choking all the time, so hard to say goodbye.
Feels like razors swallowed whole, coughing up blood, all alone.
Never wanting to let go.

Can you feel the aching in your chest?
The constriction from within, like your blood is thickening.
Can you feel the words that just won't form?
It happens all the time, wish we could just rewind.

The sudden shift in the room, it's getting to you.
Just want to run away, why can't it all just fade away?
It all just fades away.
Feel the knots in your neck.
Hanging heads low from the regret.
Wishing for one more day, maybe they would have stayed.

Can you make the words to describe the mess?
To give yourself forgiveness, you threw it all away.
Threw it all away.
And today is too damn late.
Now to live with mistake.
Living up to your own fate.

Can you feel the pressure in your throat, the words that we all know?
Its words that never leave us alone.
I just want to be alone.
Just gonna suffer on my own.
Choked up on lost hope, just couldn't let them know.
I just wish they would've known.

Can you feel the pounding in your head?
The relentless accusations, your heart tears you apart.
Never thought it would come to this.
Never wanted to make a mess.
Never got forgiveness.
Didn't want all of this.

Close your eyes to see them now, think about how it all turned out.
Had you opened up your mind, had you opened your damn mouth.
Think about the times we could have had, the times don't exist.
Never got forgiveness.
Never wanted to make a mess.

Can you feel the knots in your guts?
Think until you throw up, the ulcers are enough.
The torture never let's me get up.
It never lets up.
The smile went away, a memory of yesterday.
Should've spoke my mind, maybe I'd have you by my side.

Can you hear the voice in your head, it's your fault she ended it.
Your fault she's not alive, it's your fault she said goodbye.
As the tears burn my cheeks, all I want is to go back.
Please, I just want to go back.
I never meant to make a mess.
I hope you know you will be missed.
Hope you know you're missed.

Never wanted to make a mess.
Never gonna get forgiveness.
It all went so wrong, wish you were here with me now.
Wish you weren't forever gone.

Third Page, Third Person

All these people in all these places.
Can't avoid it, it's a sea of faces.
All these liars and deceivers.
Not twisted logic but a simple statement.

Walk the streets of all these cities.
The lights at night are all that is pretty.
Walk through crowds and all is busy.
If we had one feeling, maybe it would be amusing.

See the people and the smiling faces.
The laughter and the misbehaving.
Watch in wonder, though that black heart isn't beating.
Stand in public, drenched from the bleeding.

A sea of faces and ours remains lost in opaqueness, unseen, lost, never received.
The porcelain dolls without expression.
The 5% of society, the burden.
The ones but not worth a mention.

Alone in the crowd but always observing.
Alone in the mind, if not including the demons screaming.
The obscure are the most courageous.
Only time they get love is from all the wrong places.

Walk in the stream of the mediocre faces.
The average and the ones who think they have made it.
Live in a delusion or live in the moment.
Watch it all unfold but never a part of it.

Coping with the knowledge and deranged understanding.
Coping with life and how it's unfolding.
Coping with the knife, pills and the bottle.
The lines and the smoke that softens the blow as we hit that rock bottom.

Every second of every day coping, avoiding, subjected to pain.
Walking amongst the ones who don't understand all this "nonsense".
Live with the lost feelings, emotional carnage.
Pretending to smile and laugh, bottled emotions.
Waking each morning has become the greatest nuisance.

To You

May light show you the way.
Let your soul be guided in harmony.
Let the stars show you what no one could say.
Let their waves wash all regrets away.

May this life be shown the way.
The gift of light.
Let all heaviness be cleansed away.
The doubt and the hope are lost but can be found.

The gift of a life
From the darkness, I grant you light.
Let it be within you everyday.
Illuminated, your better side shining bright.
As the troubles fade away.

For even the day can be so bright
As I fade into the grey.
For let this be a gift
I will not accept any pay.
For when it seems there is nothing left.
Let the gift of my light show you the way.

Once more I say.
May this life be shown the way.
The gift of light.
Let all heaviness be cleansed away.
The doubt and the hope are lost but can be found.
Can be found again.

Left Turn Now

We met on that ice black night.
Two cold flames without any light in sight.
Connected in the mind.
Knowing that this cold world would tear us apart.

You talked as I soaked in the full moon's light.
All the while, asking if this could be.
If someone actually would be
A friend to me.
Joked and laughed about this life.
Philosophy and my dark insight.
Don't worry, I know I'm crazy.
That's just me, take it or let it be.

Now the days have gone and you faded out.
Left me here alone again.
Haunted by your memories.
Can still see your face.
Your fragrance, it corrupts my space.
It's been a while since you were laid to rest.

The music we shared is now a test.
The songs are stricken from my mind.
Haunted, I am inside.
Land of confusion is now my home.
I sit here still alone, destined to make it on my own.
Coma black, pounding in my head.
Love lost in a hail of gunfire is more like it.

Chelsea smile streaked across my face.
As I turn over a page of yesterday.
How could it be?
When you left, you took them from me.
The music that set me free.
Breaking the habit as I stare at the floor.
Abandon your friends as I abandon hope.
Abandon hope.
And yet I go back to that night.

You talked, as I soaked in the full moon's light.
All the while, asking if this could be.
If someone actually would be.
A friend to me.
Joked and laughed about this life.
Philosophy and my dark insight.
Don't worry, I know I'm crazy.
That's just me, take it or let it be.

Let it be.
Eventually you let me be.
And still, I am me.
So just let it be.

We met on that ice black night.
Two cold flames without any light in sight.
Connected in the mind.
Knowing that this cold world would tear us apart.
So, are you happy now?
Laid six feet underground.

Take the music and the topics shared.
Take the time spent, wasted breathable air.
Take the false pretenses.
Take the late nights now, I don't need it.
Her ghost in the fog, vanish into thick air.
Nothing left behind.
Living and pushing, in dying days.
I now part my way.

For now, the task at hand.
Is nothing less then surviving as the damned.
For now there's but one thing left.
Everything thrives in darkness.
Now I wait and bleed.
Alive out of habit.
The only numbers left.
7861 until certain death.

A Wish for Coma

Off we drift, further into the world that doesn't have to make sense.
Further we go, until the weight of the real world has no control.
Off in a dream, run with the monsters and beasts.
Off in deep sleep, perhaps it's more rainbows and fluffy sheep.

It's just peaceful in deep sleep, living a life where you don't have to be.
Living as that shadow, our other side condemned beneath our feet.
In the dream is the best thing, not having to deal with the typical.
The predictable that is but another day.

Just wish when I wake that it didn't have to be this way.
Just wish for some more sleep.
Wake up and see as the stories of our dreams fade out.
Fall away, away from me.
Nothing remains but scattered fragments, crumbled dreams.

Pieces of what never would be.
Dreams, they say, are just our brain's way of arranging memories made.
Filing each day, in some twisted ways.
Makes me smile cause of the mess that's inside.
Makes me wonder, if what I perceive as life, is actually a lie.

Pink Elephants

The lone star in the sky of groups.
The dim light in solitaire amongst the hype of constellations.
Life on the outside as I look in, this life is peaceful.
An illusion of calm.

The friends and circles, social societies creating a stress, pulling issues from
thin air.
Miss it? Not a second and I put that on my life.
It's the idea of finding some creatures that enjoy the same shit.
To redefine the term friend and bring a purpose to it.

As a light in the cosmos of all that is fucked up.
As a being with a reason.
An energy that remains so out of touch.
As a light in the cosmos.
From the other side looking in, alone and out of touch.

Drive the roads and stroll the streets.
Nothing remains, its just life on repeat.
All the parties, the criminal activities, and the delusion of importance.
Watch as the people continue the loop.
Only difference now, is I'm not part of the group.

Watch and listen to stories told, see the patterns but hold my tongue.
Watch and listen, that's the key.
If only they could do this, cycles would end.
The monotony would be a dying trend.

As a light in the cosmos of all that is fucked up.
As a being with a reason.

An energy that remains so out of touch.
As a light in the cosmos.
From the other side looking in, alone and out of touch.

Stand on the outside and look in, analyze this life and be your own friend.
The people around, they don't give a damn.
The people are lost, grabbing on to each other.
It's a wonder they all don't drown.
Hurting on the inside and using that to bring others down.
Substance abuse and crime, thinking that makes you a big man.

Full grown children running in the streets.
Full grown babies crying behind angry tweets.
Fully convinced that growing up is a myth.
Congratulations, human race.
Here's the participation award but that's all we get.

Disconnected from that rat race.
Race to the grave, the bottom moving so fast and missing all that is great.
Memories made, both good and bad.
Pushed me to just drop this shit and walk away.
Burned and been burned, it was part of the game.
Sick of playing, sick of being human.

Pulled back and became a stranger, ugly and unknown.
No one trying to be a part and no one is worth the feeling of content.
Cold as ice and head in the clouds, selfish when it comes to sharing me.
Treated like shit and abandoned; tossed to the wolves.
I didn't return or try and lead the pack.
I murdered in fashion.
Consumed all the blood.
Fuck the world and the way it doesn't work.
Free to be me and nobody has been able to keep up.

As a light in the cosmos of all that is fucked up.
As a being with a reason.
An energy that remains so out of touch.
As a light in the cosmos.
From the other side looking in, alone and out of touch.

Nameless

Saw you in a dream just the other day.
Your appearance never changes.
You always did look great.
Though the image remains only in my head.
I can't help but wonder why.
After every occurrence, you sit with me in my mind.

In life it was always adventures and good times.
But life itself is ruthless when you refuse to see through open eyes.
Life could be renewed but still, you have too much pride.

See the difference between the basic human and I.
Is that I'm my own person, in that I have no ties.
You see I keep it simple but always appear to have no time.
I keep it subtle and watch as shit gets out of line.
I dodge the social media and to messages, I often don't reply.
I guess I'm living like its still 1999.

So now it's on occasion that you stop in and say hi.
In my mind while I'm sleeping, we chill and pass the time.
I know I didn't call you and yet you still stop by.
So I take it as an omen, that someone had me on their mind.

Just know I haven't forgotten.
Not even the things I shouldn't know.
Guess having alter egos gave me more than what I thought was in store.
Hey but no worries, already opened and walked through that dungeon door.

Just out here talking to yet another ghost.
A being drifted off.

Way off course.
Good thing life is but an unscripted show.
Just a blank canvas, so to each our own.
Out of touch, perhaps purpose.
Life's a fucked up game, though I'm sure you already know.

Not Just a Feeling

Things in three is said to be but that of luck and passion.
Possess the power of the true universal attraction.
The number three is what is needed when conjuring spells of the higher powers.
Practices brought forth from the lost religion.

But the number three truly stumps me, given my life's endeavours.
The number three haunts my dreams, my days are plagued, it corrupts my being.
I swear, there is no escaping.

There is something strange, I feel pained.
Struggling, trying to decipher.
Its always three, bullshit schemes I'm subliminally apart of.
I'd say why me but I know some things that would white your wig if I tried to
turn your light on.

I have to say I'm growing bored of the strain of knowing but never talking.
I'm sure you say "then why not say just what it is you are thinking".
What if I made my decision based on shit from years before you.
Perhaps I flagged the habits unto which you've shown.
What if my efforts made are more subliminal than what you look for?

In work and play, I'm always face to face with three.
Options that get confusing.
In love and life, it's always strife, nothing out of the normal.
The plague and gift, the power of the three I'm wielding.
Maybe I have a gift, something I'm not explaining.

It's just this number three is getting a bit exhausting.
I see it, no doubt, but it's not my ball to be playing.
It's all good, maybe my third vision is the one that's coming.

If that's the case then it was too late, the plague is gonna consume you.
Always three that's consuming; three options, three people, three lives, none are simple, all I ask is for understanding.

Yeah I know we all have our own battles and fucked up demons.
But just take a seat and see; pass your heat from within your life of carnage.
Maybe it's me but a lot of you seem to have sat upon your own pedestal.
I'll be relieved when the power of three brings you back to your feet upon the ground we are walking.

It's like, ok, so you took a break but it's not ok to place yourself above us.
Humans, people as a nation.
The fuck out of here with these racial limitations.
The problem of three will be with me until I'm buried in my coffin.
I could be straight up but I'm exhausted from just breathing.
I know damn well what the deal is, now I say it's in your court because you're playing.

Eulogy of Him

Out of mind and feeling blind.
But I don't mind the irony.
Wake to sleep and sleep to awake.
This cycle never ends, monotony.

Work to find and balance time.
A life crossing the line, tolerable.
Out of mind and running blind.
Make it through the obstacles.

Some days it's hard to find.
The greatest reason why.
Everything you know, now's the time to say goodbye.
Hard to say, hard to take the truth that was never there.

It's alright, it will be fine.
Emotions likewise disappear.
Belief and hearts fade.
It all fades to grey.

Sleep to wake and wake to sleep.
Can't take another day.
Out of mind but I don't mind.
The grey is now scenery.

A bottle of pills, a bottle of chills.
The memories of yesterday.
The bottle, it kills.
Kills the feelings, indeed.

Out of mind, low on time.
The pen is to pad.
The grey turns to black.
Now it's time to embrace the blind.

Breath slowly fades.
Never had a place, let life drift away.
To live is to die and no one's gonna cry.
Out of sight, I'm out of mind.
This is the eulogy.

Out of mind and walking blind.
But I don't mind the irony.
Out of light and fade away.
The lines been drawn but no one saw.
Saw the way it affected me.

Unpopular Opinion

Opened up Facebook just the other day.
What did I see? Just another cheesy meme.
I guess them antics weren't left in 2017.
Scroll through the posts, see some diversity.
If I was you, it too would be all about me.

Self centered and retarded, another selfie? Just stop it, please.
My generation was full of misfits, Goths, wannabe gangsters, emo bitches.
We went through the motions, Manson blamed for high school shootings.
Tupac dies and the fans still cry oceans.

Freestyle motocross changing the game.
Bam and Tony were all the rage.
Music told stories; you needed talent to be noticed on the stage.
Now that's all back in the day.
Back when you rode a two stroke if you wanted to race.

Now is the era of the electronic restraint.
I looked at Insta and saw what the kids are up to these days.
Eating laundry soap isn't as good as it gets.
How about drinking four litres of bleach? Fucking degenerates.
I won't hold back just what I think.
Children raising children was the start of the downfall of the human race.

I can't help it; this shit is all over the place.
I see how the parents weren't ever raised.
I see how the system has a lot, stuck in their ways.
I see probably just the spec on the plate.
I can't help but feel saving us is a little too late.

With groups like antifa and all political campaigns.
With lower knowledge handed down, the plague passed on is the true fate.
Went from having free speech to not knowing what the fuck you just said.
Making up words, acting out, acting bad.

Copies of a copy projected by the news.
No one has a face, no one has the truth.
Eminem gave us freedom of expression, the rest us up to you.
But you failed your English lesson. Probably sitting high, in your room.
Talking bout the street but never tried on any other shoes.
I'm saying I believe we need a nuclear war zone, what about you?
I don't agree, now I'm stuck in my own zone.
It's just me being me.

I'm game for unity and all but only if you have a clue.
I'm open to friends and making some new.
But I'm done with snakes and that makes up most of you.
I have what it takes and I will push through.
Got myself; I'm on my own level, I'm not worried about you.
I'm living my life right, what's your excuse?

Hope Fades Out

Clothes scattered all around.
Just a mattress placed upon the ground.
Darkness is the living space.
Power's off, the bills aren't paid.
Clothes scattered on the ground.
Tomorrow's memories, so profound.

Lack of love, abandoned by the light.
Lost all hope but not the fight.
Lack of love, love for life.
Lost it all, nothing remains in sight.
Lack of love, low on life.
Grab my hand as I grab the knife.

Clothes scattered all around.
Just a mattress laid upon the ground.
Lack of love, lack of light.
Lack of hope, though I won the fight.
Darkness lingers all around.
Fills this body as I drown.
Leaching in as memories fade out.

Memories I cannot find.
The corruption hit delete on the better times.
Time, my old friend.
Always there but never cared.
Always there, always there.
Memories I cannot find, flashbacks of intangible times.
Time, my only friend; lead me unto death by thy own hand.
Time, so bittersweet.
Always there, always there.

Clothes scattered on the ground.
Blood soaked mattress under a body, drowned.
In the dark, never seen the light.
Bills unpaid, nothing left after the fight.
Darkness sweeps the empty streets.
Darkness slowly consuming me.

Lack of love, lack of life.
Lack of hope, though I won the fight.
Lack of love, losing sight.
Losing hope of a better life.
Lack of love, out of fight.
Take my hand as I take this knife.

Everything scattered in my mind.
Dreams, they all left my side.
Pray for life, pray for hope.
I pray for plagues as I slit my throat.
Raining loud, raining hard.
Raining blood as I hit the ground.

Saturn Lights

Hold on to the hope but feel the rope slipping.
Grip so tight, now my hands are bleeding.
Holding on to the hope, lost inside, not breathing.
It's too late in life, I can feel the pressure building.

Try to leave it behind, try to control my thinking.
But the memories seep through, the blocks I used aren't working.
Back to the book of shadows for an answer.
Back to the boards, drawing up new plans to get rid of you, miss cancer.

Back to the days where it didn't matter. Remembering because it was all together.
Back in the days of happiness found with the help of another.
Holding on subconsciously as I lay you to rest.
Tossed into the darkest fire.

Holding on to hope as hope gets smaller.
Watch the sun fade as the world feels colder.
Been a slave to this as long as I remember.
Hope holding my head, below the surface of forever.

The moment, it flashes and it's now or never.
The daylight breaks and my conscious is now fired.
For the first time in life, I no longer have desire.
The moment flashes and its now or never.

Running away with the devil.
Running away until my legs are too tired.
Wake up screaming inside because the haunting is oh so real.
Screaming inside because I don't remember how to feel.

Hollow and content is the irony I feel.
Hollow cause giving a fuck never made it on the menu.
Content with the knowledge, my importance is just not real.
Confide in me, my pretty, I'll listen as you tell me how you feel.
Confide in me, sweetie its ok, I know for me there isn't a feel.

Death and me, we got something in common.
The reaper and me, we sit, shoot the shit and occasionally cut deals.
Over the edge and beyond the horizon.
Over the mountains of depression.
The valley of death, buried in the meadow.
The part of me, my heart remains awaiting a brighter tomorrow.

Holding on to hope as hope gets smaller.
Watch the sun fade as the world feels colder.
Been a slave to this as long as I remember.
Hope holding my head, below the surface of forever.

So here I am, painting a picture.
And there you go because I never mattered.
Friends to family is like dust to ashes.
All basic chemistry but lack a feeling of real.
There we go again as I sit and listen.
Tell me how the world mistreated you.
Tell me how it is to be unhappy in a world filled with people.
Go on about friends and the issues of being social.
For I am but death, the river six's leader.
For I am unforgiven, not an option, not even a person.
For I am but what is desired.
Too good to be true, so I remain just an illusion.
Speaking from lack of existence because I'm just a bad omen.

Holding on to hope as hope gets smaller.
Watch the sun fade as the world feels colder.
Been a slave to this as long as I remember.
Hope holding my head, below the surface of forever.

Thoughts 2

I see it now, clear and loud.
What's it like to stand before this life.
Like a lost soul, too scared to knock on another door.
The labels placed from outsiders who have no place. Gaze upon them and only see a vessel, an empty space.
Friends in the past but just a stranger today.

Live, love, laugh, repeat. Some wise bullshit from the world to me.
If you find that spark, that unknown connect.
That feeling you get, that feeling from another in which you can't forget.
Pursue it and take the risk, speak from the heart, not from the perspective of dopey games.

Let's be human again, please.
Let's be a little more than just a known disease.
All this speak of equality but it's a scape goat for a different scene.
The thought of equality sounds nice like a dream but it's the hidden agenda that proves it's a slimy scheme.

Equal pay for equal work.
Equal benefits that gets tricky.
Equality is but a vision into the future.
But how are we to be equal when we're not even the same people?
Humans, just a fucked up species.
As if any one of us is any different.
Contributions and technical advances.
Lost touch with family and all that pricelessness.

I'm all for a war, an end that returns us to the Stone Age.
We lost our spark, we lost our ways.

We fight for ideas and not what's in our face.
We walk on the common man to get ahead in life like it's a race.
But we'll all be laid to rest in the same way.
Life fades in and life slips away.
Step back and appreciate the breath of the day.
Step back and reach out to the ones that make your day.
Reach out before they're gone.
Six feet under, laid away.

Return of the Witch

Burning bridges, falling down.
Falling down, falling down.
Burning friendships, fall of man.
Fall of man.
My dark angel saves us all.
Torching witches, ashes fall.
Ashes fall, ashes fall.
Releasing curses as bodies boil.
Save us all, save us all.
My dark angel hears our call.
Voices screaming, shrieks of pain.
Cries from hell.
Women and children, all have drowned.
Falling down, falling down.
Cries of pain, screaming hell.
Wives and daughters take the fall.
The cleansing begins, fear installs.
Crusades, the plagues to kill us all.
Kill us all, kill us all.
Burned at the stake.
Famine to death.
Beaten.
Drowned.
Energy shifts, jumps ship.
Comes back around.
It's a gift, it's a gift.
Bodies, the vessel in which life exists.
Practice the religion of which is the witch.
Deliver the answers in which we couldn't exist.
Protect us from darkness, save our souls.

Don't fear the stakes, there aren't even coals.
Rebuilding the bridges, restoring hope.
Return from the ashes.
Restored and renewed, return back home.
Restore the hope, restore the hope.

Light the Path

The years, they pass; feels like it didn't exist.
Time is an idea; it makes me happy thinking of a place that I do not exist.
The years, they pass; just test after test.
We live in an abyss.

Tempt me not with an idea that just doesn't fit.
I will not be trapped by your idea of how we are supposed to live.
Heaven and hell are ideas; only within us do they truly exist.
It's the law of attraction that decides in which life we will live.

Cards in a deck, pawns upon a board.
Our perception is the only thing we truly control.
Don't let the perception of wrong drown out your soul.
Take a break and reconnect with the source.

Turn off the connection with social media and break its grip.
Living in a life designed to induce stress.
Believing the news because we were told to; it is what it is.
Caught up in the energy that gains control as you feed it.

Feet upon the ground, eyes lost in the skies.
Breathe the universe in and be ok not understanding this shit.
Its part of the procedure, training the spirit.
We live in nothing, try not to complicate it.
We don't live the same lifeline, we just coexist.
We don't get exposed to the same outcomes because those pieces just don't fit.

The reaper

The sounds of hardened steel scrape against the cold floor.
The war inside is real and the battle has taken its toll.
There wont always be a tomorrow and the stories go untold.
Can hear the reaper walking.
Can hear its time to go.
Can't find the reason for the struggle.
Can't feel anything at all.
The sound, it's getting closer.
The breeze slams shut the last door.
The end is but a calling and it's time to let all hopes go.
Nothing left that truly matters, time to end the same old - same old.
Can hear the reaper walking.
Can hear its time to go.
Can't find the reason for the struggle.
Can't feel anything at all.
The sound of his scythe dragging on what was once a polished floor.
The thought of another outcome.
Before the death of hope.
The feelings that couldn't live on.
Slowly died inside, dark mind.
The breeze comes through this body.
The weathered temple of the soul.
The breeze is so gentle and yet, still so cold.
This was the desire, laid the weapons on the floor.
The war was a fun battle.
But ended the curse of being alone.
For it will only take one last moment.
The demons need to flee their home.
For the war is over now, the reaper's at the door.

Can hear the reaper walking.
Can hear it's time to go.
Can't find the reason for the struggle.
Can't feel anything at all.

Like a Vampire

Like a vampire, I seek to destroy it all.
For the love, the blood is all I know.
Like a beast, immortal and well known.
Like a vampire, I am the great unknown.

A creature of the night, darkness is my home.
Long to be alive as I devour the ones close to home.
Friends, family, lovers alike.
This infection, the darkness snuffs out the life.

If I had a penny for every bond that I broke.
I'd buy myself a ticket, passage to hells door.
If I had the heart you think still exists.
Exists within these bones.
I'd take the chance and ask for passage.
Forgiveness for all the wrong.

I'm the creature that lurks behind closed door.
I had a vision, but destruction is all I know.
Like a vampire, blood lust and hollow.
In this darkness is my home.
I lurk in the dungeon as I wish for something more.

Existing like a shadow, a stain that just won't go.
The bane of insecure, so I remain the great unknown.
The time stopped counting once the monster gains control.
The greatest disappointment, I am the greatest unknown.
If I had a penny for every bond that I broke.
I'd buy myself a ticket, passage to hells door.
If I had the heart you think still exists.

Exists within these bones.
I'd take the chance and ask for passage.
Forgiveness for all the wrong.

Harbour all the evil as I slit another throat.
I will embrace the way they made me.
I'll gladly take another soul.
Like a vampire, I am the darkest of unknown.
The darkness inside me is the closest thing to home.
Blood thirsty vengeance, hatred for all human.

I can alter your own thoughts, I twist the weaker mind.
Install self doubt and destroy the twinkle in your eye.
A creature to be feared, created by the hatred of mankind.
Only thing that saves me has already slipped away.
Like trash in the alley, like a filthy stray.
A product of the torment, forged in betray.

Nothing!

Infected bag of flesh that's beating.
Your words alone won't save this being.
Into the nothing is where you'll find me.
If you venture, if you love me.
Take my hand, tear me from the demons.

As I suffocate on words unspoken.
Wade into the waters, unto deception.
The black waters of all that is broken.
I can't find a purpose, can't find a reason.
In the waters, submerged in treason.
As the infection slows my breathing.
Drowning, gasping, choking, bleeding.
As you stand there cross armed and smiling.

I look right at you and you see nothing.
You've shown me only what you wanted.
Your mouth of lies, webs your weaving.
The gothic romance, my Juliet.
Pinned me down, under glass.
Tear me away from myself.
Ignore my feelings, you redirect.
I love you but you love nothing, theft!

This infected bag of flesh, still beating.
I'm on my knees upon this alter.
Feel the presence of the water.
Craving the touch of another.
I crave your presence, I crave your laughter.
I can see you smile in the darkness.
Follow me to my monsters.

Come and find me if you love me.
Only you know how to save me.
Not with your words, but with your body.
Show me I have your company.

Choking on words left unspoken.
I choke on them as I force a smile.
I'm drowning in this losing battle.
The war of life wages inside me.
I feel the infection growing wild.
I look at you, but I see nothing!
You only show me your deception.
Filled me with false hope as you stabbed me.
Knife in my back as you held me.
Satan's smile is your weapon!
Eyes ocean blue and your beauty!

In my eyes, so close to perfect.
All your flaws and all your bitching.
Your battles and hidden depression.
In the undertones of all that's spoken.
I see it but will never use it against you.
You kill me but I adore you!

The infection stops my breathing.
Lungs of blood and I'm drowning!
I reach for you, for some comfort.
You're not here, left with nothing.
You bleed me dry with all the stabbing.
Are you happy?
Pinned with a smile.

Are you accomplished in your conquest?
A gothic romance that was one sided.
A tomb stone that reads nothing.
I reached for you, I reached for nothing!
My curse is being human.
Body, casket, tombstone, nothing! nothing!
Blank rock marking lack of existence!
Nothing!

Now You Know, But You Don't Care

I woke from my dream, confused of my location.
I dreamt of you again, another piece to a puzzle.
This time was different though.
You gave me the cold shoulder.

Now I have awakened from what feels like forever.
Living in two worlds is how it truly feels.
Like life when I'm dreaming and a life worth nothing.
Like sitting in the back seat, a car with no destination.

If I kissed you in one world, do you feel it in the other?
Or is it just more shit, more disappointment?
Is it just monotonous, calling future from present?
This is all bullshit, the pendulum of forever.
Life is torture set in perpetual motion.

We go months without any connection.
Conversation ends without any question.
I support each and every one of your decisions.
I watch from the sidelines and listen to your story.
I see how you bounce around in a bi polar commotion.

That's just me being this kind of person.
That is about the most of my time I have given.
Not enough, never gonna be noticed.
These efforts to me are just basic friendship.
If only you could feel this energy I carry.
If you could only feel the breath of my dragon.

But that's ok cause I got you in that other dimension.
The fun we have and all the adventure.
You're missing out, maybe I'm just delirious.
I'm missing life, days of heightened happiness.
I gave up the drugs and even my prescriptions.
I changed my life up, but you wouldn't know it.
If being me is not enough then I won't approach you.
Just wait for the dreams, the place where I hold you.

Unicorn Shit

I raise my hand to hers.
You are the bearer of all that is light.
Emotions entangled, a mess that feels right.
You chase away the darkness.
Extended purpose of this life.

Hand in hand, together.
As we walk the streets at night.
You rest upon my shoulder.
Cause I will keep you safe with my life.
Love, it comes too easy.
When I gaze into your eyes.

When it comes to life in the future.
All I see is her and I.
I still have some depression.
But for her, I set it aside.
No need for explanation.
In each other, we confide.

Long walks in the evening.
To even longer drives.
With her there is no exception.
We will do it all before we die.
For her I'll show emotion, for her I'll go another mile.

Even when we argue, throw venom with our words.
We push each others' buttons.
But we always make amends.
Through the darkest hours.
We will be together in the end.

I'm in love with an angel.
A demon in the bed.
She looks at me in wonder.
Traces scars with fingertips.
Asks a million questions.
She will never give up.

Long walks in the evening.
To even longer drives.
With her there is no exception.
We will do it all before we die.
For her I'll show emotion, for her I'll go another mile.

I sit in wonder as she sleeps.
Life was pure evil.
Until the gift of you, I received.
You are my perfect partner.
An oasis from my pain.
You are my happy ending.
Acquired position of best friend.

All these songs we know, and together we always sing.
If I could stop the time.
With you, I would repeat the day.
If I could read your mind.
You would do the same.

Long walks in the evening.
To even longer drives.
With her there is no exception.
We will do it all before we die.
For her I'll show emotion, for her I'll go another mile.

Odd One

The moments we endure are the stories we have to tell.
But what do you do when all you have is music and your shadow upon the wall?
Laying awake, listening to the same songs.
Lay awake and go over all the times you did wrong.

A social butterfly with wings clipped.
A friendly being so misunderstood.
Hear the voices in the background, the angels in your head.
Calling out for a chance, "you just need to get out of your head".

But the dust covers your body.
Your heart is on the shelf.
Your voice is damaged, you can barely speak at all.
You came to terms with your life.
All the terrible things that you did.
You are better off alone.
Trapped between forgotten and dead.

The people rush together; its a beautiful sight.
The friends and the gatherings.
Like fireflies in the night.
The songs are so happy.
So perfectly flawed.
You witness all the laughter as you watch from afar.

Acid tears burn the face of an angel in the dark.
The memories of a time, a place from before.
What you want is all you had.
Been down this road before.
The sirens sing the most beautiful songs.

Plagues of a butterfly captive, within dungeon walls.
The light doesn't enter, and the windows are bars.
Lost in forever until you forget who you are.

The silence is broken only by your songs.
If music was not an option, you would have nothing at all.
So, you sit and you scream along with the songs.
Write and you write but only garbage comes out.
Play with the volume to drown what's inside your head.
Play with all the letters of the alphabet.

Dust covers your body, angels called it quits.
Tears long dried up, you no longer give a shit.
Years of isolation, they call it neglect.
Pinned with depression because they just don't get it.
Scars on your body look desperate.
If only they knew it was reassurance.
That ability to commit.

Suddenly you hear the hustle.
The sound of content.
You smell the perfume, reminds you of some chic.
The energy shifts as you bask in the doom.
You close your eyes and pretend that they are you.

The people rush together; its a beautiful sight.
The friends and the gatherings.
Like fireflies in the night.
The songs are so happy.
So perfectly flawed.
You witness all the laughter as you watch from afar.

You remember a place.
A time you had it all.
You embrace and reconsider your fault.
What if this place, where once was your heart.
Could recalibrate, could carry on.
The world forgot, your friends are long gone.

You stepped back and the world carried on.
All that you know is in all of those songs.
Sit and you think of all you did wrong.
Until its too late and your spirit is gone.

S.S.D.D

Like a moth and the flame
Tragedy crosses us again
Hidden truths deep within
The ocean of lies
Forced to swim

The fire to the fly
Escape is but a lie
Cope and carry on
Knowing the cycle
The depressive, entitled

Same day, same day
Moments fall away
Same place, not again
See past all that's dim
Same pain, different place
That name haunts the brain

Chase the sun, catch the light
Chase dreams, day and night
The cycle repeats but with wisdom

It can be beat
Same day, different song
Longing for someone to sing along
This place in the heart
The same place that fell apart
The hatred for fellow man
Will it ever be whole again?

Like a moth to the flame
The fly that sets skies ablaze
The happiness we all chase
The love we embrace

Same day, different ways
Coping as we walk through another daze
The cycles, tests and hell
Build us up and tear us down
We walk, hand in hand
The creatures of the damned
There is no one around
But we all walk on common ground

Like a moth to the flame
Like the past recirculates
The tears and the blood
The tests, don't give up
The people will run you down
But face to face, don't make a sound
Your friends are within your head
The only one who gives a shit
The trust is but a myth
If I gave it away, I'd have nothing left

Like the fire to the fly
Illuminate your dreary sky
Reconnect with what's inside
Reconcile, have some pride
Same day, different way
Another shot at yesterday
The people will bring you down
Don't lose your heart
Swim until you drown
Until the sun washes away
Oxidizes the memories
Be your own best friend
Stand behind what you believe in

Another Star in The Web of Forever

Three years of pain, finally the sun broke the rain.
Alone but not ashamed; three years and a day.
It's too bad I don't belong like yesterday.
Dreams of her but, who is she?
Taking up space, assuming my place.
The sidelines of life, as I watch everyone fall away.

Three years but feels like yesterday.
No, not the pain or a fucking deranged memory.
This is about me recovering my pride and some sanity.
I lost it all when I laid with the devil.
I gave up on friends, believing in forever.
Tried to be me while bending for another.

See, this is the reason I socially retired.
I took those words and made it a forever.
Now I get patrolled and stalked but it's like, whatever.
I shut down harder than ever.
I left the province and tried to re discover.
My purpose, my soul and even my smile.

Three years but now I feel like it's over.
I don't know where I fit.
Love? What is it? I don't remember.
I've been friend zoned like it doesn't matter.
I have endured the extortion and subliminal backstabbing, the rumours.
Friends were just enemies, lesser humans with jealous agendas.

I was living in rock bottom for what feels like forever.
I was waiting for the storm to break, awaiting something better.

I saw the sun for the first time, and it didn't feel much better.
No longer in pain, no but I'm still a fucking loner.
No longer guarded but now no one is even looking.
Ready to try and continue this puzzle.
Trapped by my brain and twisted humor.
Ugly but wise, its a package deal.

I give my time and watch as you waste it.
I try really hard to be a social person.
I speak but no one listens.
I answer the phone calls, that's actually a big deal.
The rain lifted, I can now bask in surreal.
The sun broke the storm, now I want more than my shadow.

Acid Tears

Somewhere between real and pretend
Trust was broken, you lost a friend
All that's left are memories
Shared memories trigger the acid tears

Acid tears sooth the eyes
Leaking dust and wasting time
Scar your face and kill the pride
Acid tears never dry

Sit and watch as time goes by
Sit in limbo under a pregnant sky
Hope you ponder and reconcile
That it haunts and robs your smile

All the times you sit alone
Hear my voice in your undertones
Residue of my presence within your head
Lessons taught and words unsaid

As acid tears soothe the eyes
Leaking dust and passing time
Dissolving love and killing pride
Acid tears never dry

Hurt gets worse as days go by
Burns more with each tear you cry
Every word ever said
Resonates within your head
Reverberates until your dead

Family calls and friends check in
Sleep evades, impending doom
Bottles scattered all around
Three-month prescription is long gone

Convulsions raging out of control
Body arched, breaking bones
Light fades out as heart rate peaks
Eyes roll back, lightning strikes

Open casket, your mother cries
Acid tears fill her eyes
Leaking dust and wasting time
Scar her face and kill the pride
Acid tears that never dry

Days move on as they did before
Only difference is the remorse
The memories left inside your head
The memories of a friend now dead
Days move on, you continue to age
Acid tears damaged your face

All you see when they say "back then"
Is that one person, the truest friend
All you think when the memories play
What would they have been like on this very day?
As acid tears roll back in
Down your cheeks and burn your chin
As you lay down to rest
As you choke down each breath

A family torn from hurt, depressed
All move apart and avoid the mess
Friends, the people that say they miss
Wish the time spent was more permanent
At the grave each and every year
Flowers laid, drenched in acid tears

Soft Thinking

Soft thoughts and well wishing
Reduced to minimal but still thinking
On my mind and in visions
Nothing's changed, just my playlist

Soft thoughts, pretty faces
No matter the frustration
No matter the distance
I remain, my eye on the target

I tried to talk to others
Good conversation but something's missing
No matter the topic
No matter the person

Wish it was you who was getting my attention
I see you in my mind, a picture so perfect
Strange how the aura and spirit can connect so deep and feel magnificent

Heart beat races and the world stops spinning
Words deteriorate and I fumble my sentence
Had a hard time understanding why it's so different
Why I get so nervous and miss communicate, trying to reply to a message

This is the purest of my emotion
Never in my life have I spent so much time well wishing
Never have I had someone in my mind, in so many visions
Never have I lost my words and felt so stupid

Its been a while but I still miss you
Nothing's changed, I can't replace you
I try and make friends and talk to people
Maybe you noticed, maybe you viewed me
Just know it's a social experiment
I can't seem to care about any others

I only see you when I focus
Guess my heart's an asshole
And my mind kind of wanders
But every single day I think of you and this devotion
Maybe it's futile but I won't make excuses
I know I'm wise, but I feel kind of stupid
Maybe I tend to read too deep into it?

It's like this, everyone knows I'm a wordsmith
My ability with this language is fairly ambitious
But when someone says something that could have more than one meaning
My brain and feelings go off the deep end

I know how I want to take it
But reason and logic keep my hopes in the basement
I doubt myself and I doubt intuition
I guess I'm so smart I'm stupid?

It's like my clear quartz heart
Polished and imperfect
Flaws that captivate, some intrusive
Still whole and real, pure but slightly elusive
Of all descriptions, definitely not useless
Complex but simple and full of greatness
Marks left from being ambitious
Head shy because everything now seems ambiguous

So really not so stupid, so full of hindsight
It becomes confusing
Too many times, repeated situations
Unfortunately, I'm shy from abusive relations
I really do try and push through it

The best I've got is what is given
My issue is my overactive imagination
My doubt based off prior deceptions

I get lost in my thoughts like it is inception
Thought within a thought and so on
Next thing I know, my readings are fiction
Back track and try to determine
The whole time I'm just cycling emotions
Laugh and cry, anger and disappointment
Sometimes I just really need someone to bring me to the surface
Let me know I'm ok, that I'm in the right direction

But I am alone and the years keep on counting
Not complaining, just making a statement
No one has even remotely taken an interest
Not sure why, maybe I angered the wrong people
Either way, it doesn't make a difference
Cause I love me and I'm still well wishing

I embrace all the memories and all the shared experience
You truly have a place in my deepest storage
I don't care, I'm willing to admit it
My intent was end game, fuck all the searching
I worked on me and found you in the process
Maybe I erased a thousand unsent messages
Maybe I missed key hints and moments
But I can't live in the maybe or it will kill me

Just know I still think of you
I still care and all that good stuff
Forever a friend because that is important
Everyday I wish you well and whisper my statements
Let the wind take them with some wishful thinking
Asking the universe to deliver and trust you receive them

And with respect, you will remain nameless
I'm just passing time, going through the motions, writing out emotions
Almost lost all of my interests, had to reconnect with my spirit

No matter what way I look at it
I remain, still here, well wishing
That piece that I never knew was missing
Tears on my cheeks as I peak through the fences
I just hope you don't forget me
Is this the final chapter?
Setting the record straight, soft thinking
A break from giving voice to the darkness
Hopefully you enjoyed this installment

All I've got now is knowing my emotions
Knowing that I have found my feelings
Existing and loving from a distance
Not lust, trust me, I already contemplated the possibility
This is something totally new, lacking a description aside from unique
Guess only for one, I wear this heart on my sleeve
Cause the rest of them can't get a single fuck from me
That's another way I can tell it is real
I don't know, it's just how I feel
Soft thinking

I Miss

Creative words and skills for building.
Capable hands and a knowledgeable being.
Wondered to and from the darkest of corners.
Pondered life's meanings and questioned its purpose.
Dissecting this mysterious world around me.
At an age where you were all children still playing carefree.

Been down the roads of every emotion.
Feels like three lifetimes I've lived in.
I don't know how to exist with what I have been given.
I don't want to be an extraterrestrial being.
To be seen as that much different.
I don't like that I'm a disposable comfort.
That I tend to be to logical and monotonous.
Believe it or not, I'm extremely light hearted.
But sometimes I miss the punchline and kill the humor.

It hurts me to receive so much spurning.
To be labelled as nothing short of cranky.
Described as irritable and angry.
Viewed as depressed and unhappy.
I do not believe that best describes me.
I feel like I am worthy, I feel content and yes, even happy.
I just forget to wear it physically.
Maybe its because I'm so deep in lonely.
How many years would you last if this was your story?
The way I have been treated and all the extortion.
I bend over backwards even when I can't afford it.

I struggle a lot, but I remain silent.
Being strong because no one can help me.
Trying to be a friend even when I see I mean nothing.

Long hours and I continue to stay willing.
How many times I dropped everything.
Cancelled my own ambitions, promptly.
What about the late nights I sat up and listened.
How about all the tears I swallowed in the name of forgiveness.
Even when I hurt and wanted to end it.
I still give my hand, love and knowledge.

No one ever stopped to wonder.
Took a second to think above it or acknowledge how hard I've been trying.
But everyone knows me for not smiling.
For being the downer and not complying.
For keeping myself trapped at the bottom.
It's my fault that all I get is rejection.
It's my fault that I'm bound in silence, the suffering is my own doing.
It's my fault I'm below most desired, feels like the bar is set beyond what I aspired.

Yet, I wake up every morning no matter how tired.
Wish the best and keep trying.
I laugh and I joke in the moment.
I teach and I learn without being biased.
I miss, and that's been a new constant.
I want nothing but good for every human.
Even the retards that from me, deserve nothing.
The ones who speak negative about me.
The ones who take advantage and drain me.
The ones who forget all about me, I'm still surprised no one has checked on me.

Ya, I have a history, I have grown up with severe depression.
But I don't let that define me, I refuse to let it.
It makes me sad that no one gets me.
That I reach my hand out and there is nothing.
That I remained living, to be alone no matter what I'm trying.
I'm sorry but it isn't worth it.
I deserve more than this sick punishment.

The voices have been calling.
They say I was wrong about trying.
I was wrong about remaining.
That I wasted time and wasted energy.
They tell me I am worthless.
That if I held value, this wouldn't be my circumstance.
They tell me how to do it.
They beg and plead me to go through with it.

I'm at a loss with intuition.
I'm worth a lot but feels like no one sees it.
6000km from any interest.
How the fuck am I supposed to feel, aside from useless?
I'm not perfect and I have my secrets.
I was told to vanish, so I did it.
But now I'm left alone and fading.
There is a lot more to this bullshit story.
But I'm losing interest and motivation.

I try and not focus and try and forget it.
The things I say to some people.
It's better if I neglect my feelings.
I'm tired of being monitored, hacked phones and the deceiving.
And again, the demons reach me.

Tell me that I'm wanted dead and that's why they push me.
Tell me to slit my throat and fade to nothing.
I never thought I'd feel so hated.
I never thought this would be my meaning.
Hang me from the trusses and just beat me.
I'm probably one of the purest humans.
I'm a punching bag, just taking a beating.

See I like to mimic, to match little fibs and see where it takes us.
But I'm guilty of having some filthy habits.
The things I'd do if it ever came down to it.
Not the type to talk about, so I tend to just speak in bullshit.
Hoping that things work out and I get to show it.
But that's working against me.
If I mimic them, then no one gets to know me.

Then I seem like a prude and get scrapped in judgment.
It's hard trying to accept my outcome.
It's even harder remembering where I come from.
I think I may have an answer.
Think I'm gonna sell my shit and bail.
Passport over open water.
I'm way too adapting to fail.
This life I have isn't concrete, I'm not bound to it by any means.
Maybe I can outrun this hardship.
Maybe I can die in a place no one knows me.

If I Don't Wake Up

Sit and ponder, ask if life has come and gone.
No one left to lean on; a bird without a song.
Asking the powers, creatively, to forgive all my wrongs.
Constricted by these vices; the phrases of broken songs.
Lyrics pouring out of me, can't turn the fountain off.

And if I don't wake up, and the nightmare carries on.
I'll be trapped, stranded within another hell.
If I never wake up, it won't matter much at all.
Either way, I seem to be the burden; trash tossed out by you all.

Trying to resonate something in myself.
Asking karma if my debts have been paid in full.
I ask again; will she forgive all of my wrongs?
I designed this life I lead to be the best I can.
But this life, it seems, forgot I'm still around.
Sit and ponder, ask if life has come and gone.

Feel like a blank space; existing without a cause.
When I look back, I see faces of people once so close.
When I think back, I see the patterns like a spiders webs, weaving in and out.
Remember connect the dots?
Pictures just appear.
Remember the time we spent, the times you said you care?
I remember things once said and the actions as time moved on.

It's a nightmare for me, a burden that I can't turn off.
It's like the hands of time for me are moving slow.
What you say and do show who you truly are.
You can lie to you, but I will always see what you truly are.

Not judgemental, just disappointed.
Where did it go wrong?

So, I sit and ponder, ask if life has come and gone.
If this is my punishment for a past life I filled with wrongs.
I can't relate to the average man.
It sickens me, the "culture" that we're in.
I'm against the grain; black and white with how I live.
I wish someone would step up.
Never meant to seem above you all.
I can't help it if out of life, I just wanted something more.

And if I don't wake up, and the nightmare carries on.
I'll be trapped, stranded within another hell.
If I never wake up, it won't matter much at all.
Just another day for me, just a bird without a song.

Is this my destiny, has life for me already come and gone?
Sentenced to purgatory, no one asking how I am.
Feels like punishment, knowing I'm not loved.
Not a stab at family, cause they don't have a choice.
Just speaking my reality, the one thing that I know.

Just hard to grasp, being an undesired soul.
Maybe it's me, but I'm kind of picky who I call.
Doesn't mean I won't give it some time and try.
But if it doesn't trigger my heart from its hole.
I won't waste any time like I did the times before.
Guess I realised what I want, and I deserve to be acknowledged, not trolled.

It's Over

(Sometimes dwelling on what was becomes a toxic habit
that steals years from your what could be)

Lesser than my better half and still better than your upper hand.
Tell me, how does that give you a winning hand?
Haven't you had enough?

Well, I have.

I think it's funny how I did this all alone.
But you needed stepping stones.
Using people to make you feel worthy.

Or something...

Don't the games get old? Don't you see your mistakes with the work you've
shown?
Cause in the end, you're the one to pay.
Haven't you noticed?

Karma.

And all the victims would have walked away.
Made their peace and had better days.
Leaving you faded, a memory slowly dying.

Dying.

Left in the shadows, in the yesterday.
That unnoticeable distraction.

I was there in the flesh, I was true and never jessed.
Never let myself get caught up or captured.

And I'm thankful.

I let my guard down a little bit.
Just enough to catch a glimpse.
To see just what it is you're made of.
I heathed the warnings, but in the end.
Just see you as hurting, just like a child.

And that kills me.

Now time has passed and there isn't a second guess.
Nothing that keeps me up, no thinking.
Nothing left.
All I know is the mess and the drugs that left me faded.
Back in my youthful days, before I had an adult perspective.
Thought I made it.

Sure, there is memories, stories that make me laugh.
But the trauma wasn't worth it.
So, I walked away, and I doubt you regret it.
In the end it was nothing short of disappointment.

The usual.

And these thoughts just come; yesterday, I finally found my closure.
I don't hate you but what you did was beyond forgiveness.
No, I don't hate you and I know the part I played made it easy.
Should've thrown the towel in when I had them visions.
Let my guard down to a sucker punch.

I was jaded.

No longer willing to ignore it.
Lesser than my better half but better than your upper hand.
I'm out here and I'm hungry, pursuing happiness.
I keep moving on, never looking back.

I learned from that betrayal.
So, I pick the pieces up and learn to not give up.

Give up.

Still would like an answer.
Sometimes friends don't work out.
Sometimes they just drag you down.
Everything but loyal.
But that's the price that's paid.
For being made of greatness and better things.
It's not our fault, we're the ones who stand out.
Being better than they're able.
My words of wisdom for you.
Not an ounce of hate will bring back those lost days.
So, don't look back.
Just keep your head up.
And keep trekking through the forest.

You got this.

Its not your fault they couldn't see, pushed you away like you meant nothing.
Let them suffer.
It's over.

Over.

Dark Crown

Nothing left in memory, it's just ruins on the ground.
Nothing left to hold me back.
Hold me from having hope.

Nothing left in memory, the old me that I drowned.
Nothing left to hold me back.
Hold me from having hope.
Cleanse this mind in darkness, the place I hold the crown.

Nothing left to fear, feet placed firmly on the ground.
Nothing left but black and I see.
The lost that can be found.
I found myself in darkness and I fought for my crown.

Lost in the desert, death scattered all around.
Lost but still alive, you see.
Its not me, not me I need to find.
It's just me, just me against my mind.
Lost in the desert, sifting sands of time.
Lost all my walls today; Berlin falls again.

It's just me; it's just me and father time.
Nothing left in memory.
Thoughts of what went wrong.
Habits left in ruins.
Ruined by my hands.

Left it on the table and politely stepped away.
One step back, not gone forever.
Just trying to be a better me.
This isn't my best yet.

Like all that is unknown.
I sit in my peace and listen to my soul.
It's just me, myself, and I climbing from the deepest hole.

Sifting the sands of time.
Waiting for the story to unfold.
Comfort comes at night.
Watching stars in the cold.
Summon self forgiveness, make peace with what's been done.
If the demons won't leave, they will be consistent friends.
Yes, aim for self forgiveness, make peace with what's been done.
If the demons won't leave, they will be consistent friends.

It's just me; it's just me and father time.
Nothing left in memory.
Thoughts of what went wrong.
Habits left in ruins.
Ruined by my hands.
Easier to seek forgiveness, they say.
Or just don't bite the fucking hand.
It's me again; just me and father time.
Just another day, another reason to start again.

Cleanse this mind in darkness, the place I hold the crown.
Nothing left to fear, feet placed firmly on the ground.
Nothing left but black and I see.
The lost that can be found.
I found myself in darkness.
I fought for my crown.

So, hold your judgement.
Cause I know who I am.
Or you can join me.
Take my beaten hand.
King of the shadows, ruler of that land.
Master of these demons.
They are consistent friends.
So, hold your judgement.
Cause I know who I am.
Yeah, I know who I am.

Hope

A life lacking purpose.
Every shard of hope, shattered.
What is expected is far from what's given.
Trapped in a conscious unclear.
No longer know the definition of fair.
No longer believe in a heaven.
What is a safe place when the voices fuckin hate you?

A life lacking purpose.
A child battles depression.
Tell me what's fair and I'll show you what isn't.
Show me a purpose, a reason to be hurting.
Offer more fables, more advice that life is what we make it.

Push through and block out the internal sickness.
Dry heaving, not eating, crying, searching for some purpose.
Religion always failed to give viable answers.
People always seemed to steer clear because of the illness.
Depression, anxiety, Bipolar disorder, so many labels.
The episodes of mania that leaves one sleepless.
Poor decisions made by that hyper active perspective of "fuck it".
Rash decisions from the most clouded of judgment.
Leaves one with memories best left neglected.
So many pills eaten by the fist full.
Angry for being depressed and having no reason.
Depressed because you want to have fun, but your mind is off in the distance.

Falling in love but fearing rejection.
The fear is driven by lack of friendships.
Lack of friends because of being a depressive.

Depressed and not having a reason.
Paying attention to all the things people are saying.
Being traded off for a friend because of the smile you're lacking.
Lacking the smile because inside your crying.
Crying inside because you just want to feel normal and accepted.
Craving to smile and the light-hearted fun having; things that are just a shard of a memory.

Years turn to decades; the shit never gets easier.
The therapists lied when they said they can fix you.
They give you the idea that all this is beneath you.
Inflate your mind and expand your ego.
But it never lasts, it never gets easier.
Your mind has been damaged from the pills that you've eaten.
Your perspective is broken and stuck in the hole, the only place you feel comfortable.

A life lacking purpose and nothing is saving.
Can't save yourself when you don't know how else to be living.
Can't break the cycles no matter how many ways you attempt it.
Comes back down to that negative perception.
Either numb and not caring, or on the verge of a breakdown.
Try to be true to feel your feelings, but it rushes you like a release of endorphins.
Clouds your judgement and your social interpretations.

A life lacking purpose.
A feeling that giving up would be so much more than worth it.
But you wake up each day, trying to get past it.
To scream over the voices, to not think so negative.
Wake up each morning with the intent to beat it.
To get what your heart desires.
Even if you get knocked out, beaten by the bully.
The evil in your head that you have been forced to live with.
You offer your heart, friendship and forgiveness.
Flip the tables and try and feel their side of the fences.
You understand how you become part of the problem.

The people you don't like are a dime a dozen.
Everything you never wanted, it's a fucking disaster.

You work your ass off to be a certain person.
Master your mind and understand when it's just the depression.
Master the language so you can explain your emotion.
Laid the blueprints for the dream you never stopped chasing.
Almost giving up so many times, can count the scars to prove it.
But you got up and pushed through every sad illusion.

Decades of this torment have now doubled.
How many times has the same cycle looped over?
Approach it in different ways just like you've been instructed.
Maybe it's not you, it's them and the way they've been treated?
Maybe you are the only good person.
Maybe no one else gives a shit about who they are hurting?
Maybe they get their kicks out of the pain they're inflicting.
Maybe it truly is the suicide season.
To escape all the bullshit.
To be how you're feeling.
What's the difference between living and feeling?
Hated, then just straight up not existing.
You'll know who cared by who shows up to the funeral.

But you can't do that because you're not a quitter.
Give up on everything but life, cause fuck it.
Shit is a gift and you damn well accept it.
Maybe the cards never play out perfect.
Maybe you are in pain in every moment.
Maybe you just want to be needed.
Maybe it never happens, but if you're not there, you will never see it.
The catch 22, the pinnacle moment.
Too wise to not be curious, to stupid to end it.

Out of Words

Ran out of words.
Out of lines.
Out of air.

Collapsed are the lungs as you choke on despair.
Villain of love, can't kill what isn't shared.
Seconds to hours, days turn to years.

Long patients, black clothes.
Fogged mind and long hair.
High hopes surely faded; sober, but still wasting tears.

Blades to the throat, needles stitched up neat.
Drugs screaming my name, alcohol repeats.
Gave it up looking for retreat.
But you wouldn't know, just another pigeon on the street.

Guess when I cared, you started tearing at the seams.
Guess when I tried, you decided to fuck with me.
My mind like a game, but you just pushed me away.

Out of words.
Out of lines.
Out of air.

One strike; avoiding me and lying to my face.
Two strikes; I needed you, my friend, I needed emotional release.
Conversation stops as soon as you get me to speak.
Three strikes; this is about the gift.
3 years since I gave anything and what did I get?

More lies to my face, but It's not personal, you claimed.
Look me in the eyes next time and I may believe what you say.
Still to this day, don't know if you even opened it, or if in the trash it was laid.

Skies lit.
Sunsets.
Moon's full but has passed.

To what do I owe
Depression turned to anger, as outward I lash.
Treat me like I don't have a clue.
How many times have I said: games are something I don't do?

Turn the tables, walk in these worn out shoes.
No one is calling, no one is caring; alone in everything you do.
No one trying, no interest in joining all you pursue.

Caring is something sacred, not anyone can trigger in you.
Pushing through barriers and inducing anxiety attacks to prove you truly care.
Physical illness and sleepless nights drag on.
None of it means a goddamn thing because they refuse to see.
Refuse to acknowledge and you struggle to breathe.

Out of words.
Out of lines.
Out of air.

Yeah, I love you, but this isn't fair.
This bullshit is childish, and no one is worth becoming ill.
If you love someone back, then let it show.
It's called being an adult, stop living in grade 4.

Fucking with a dark mind and caged-in soul.
Count yourself fucking lucky it didn't end with blood on the floor.
Blood on your hands cause it would be made known.

Memory in photograph, just like how you know every song.
I work in hindsight and I see what you do.
I could pick you apart and destroy your excuse.

No worries, I'm bigger than you.
No worries, the scars will remind me of you.
No worries, I now know I never meant anything to you.
No worries, I'll kill myself from your life cause that's what you wished me to do.
Loved you more than anything and was beyond patient with you.
I showed you plenty of my uncaged soul.
When you grow up a little, come knock on my door.

Step Up

Long nights spent thinking.
Lost time but, not really.
See, there is a catch to being authentic.
Some say, " If I could do it over, man, I'd do it different".
Separate space and time, tear into the fabric.
Take back a twisted line or go to a specific moment.

Although I'm sure the idea inclines a perfect ending.
But for me, I feel it really makes no difference.
I sat in the dark and talked to spirits.
I walk this path, haunted upstairs by the demons.
Had some nightmares that got too close to real.
Night terrors, paralyzed, not even breathing.

All these hours invested into self interpretation.
Mastering my mind before it fucking kills me.
Finding placement of "the line" and trying not to cross it.
Found out who I truly am and have since stuck with it, knowing I'd fight for mine
when it comes down to it.

There is no crime in being authentic, for writing all these lines and meaning every
word in it.
But to go back?
I would, but only to relive it.
I wouldn't change a thing, I couldn't do it different.
If I chose another way, added another adverb to a sentence.
It would be a lie and I couldn't live with it.
See, every interaction and opinion given, that was me being as real as you're ever
gonna get.

Maybe I set myself up for another failure?
No that can't be it, even second place gets some silver.
Element that I drape around my neck, granting spiritual protection.
Last time I checked, my dragon said I'm winning.
Maybe not in the physical, maybe something's missing.

Working with energies, not being a shitty person.
Morning rituals and you know I'm still well wishing.
I'm casting out into the never-ending darkness, I find it within me to give forgiveness.
Sleepless nights and psychic visions.
Its ok though, tears only take up collective moments.

Night terrors, waking up breathless.
Seeing the tall man staring from the corners.
Seeing the demons scratching ruins into doorways.
Viscous attacks formed from words of hatred towards me from another.
Kinda feels like I have a fan, a jealous follower.

Maybe it's how I am, the lyricist and a teacher.
Maybe I'm oblivious of how their partner likes me.
What if I crossed a line by being too good of a person?
The irony in that has my mind in fucking stitches.
Like, copy me all you want, but you're never gonna make it.
Occult on my side and I'm a strong believer.
Magic, music, spirit and sharp intuition.
I'm aware that my beliefs come from a matriarchy system.

I'm aware that the ego is huge in spite and it's a given.
That anger and letting things build, an internal pressure.
Traps the being in a ruthless cycle.
Model yourself after the premise of another?... no.
Where are your interests? Where are you going?
I'm just doing me and balancing my energy, I love from every chakra in me.
Not afraid to say it, or to let it run through me.

I'm authentic and I stand behind me.
I am not afraid, you're never gonna beat me.
I'm manifesting everyday, turning imagination into reality.

Consciously controlling my sacred energy.
So, the next knock on my door, I will be ready; divine timing and tarot cards have told me.
See me in the streets, I'd suggest not trying to fight me.
See me in your dreams, I'll be the one smiling.

So, if I could go back and do it over.
I'd do it the same, maybe hug a little longer.
But everything I ever said, would still be.
Just like the things I wrote about; that someone once special to me.
Hidden within a book and filed, unreleased, for only they should see.
It's this little thing I like to call energetic decency.
I think you need some soap to wash away the black energy.
Stop falling for guilt, you have a higher energy.
They need to stop manipulating minds, that shit disgusts me.

Ever Loved?

Ever love someone so much you don't get in the way, just let feelings pile up?
Ever care about the what is, and the what ifs keep you up?
To be supportive and sacrifice everything deep inside.
To lend a listening ear as the voices rage inside.

Ever love someone, no conditions on this shit.
Like you keep hurting me with all this pettiness.
I can't offer you my heart, I can't be honest in my part.
I can't tell you how I feel and how you keep fucking up my heart.

Ever feel so helpless, like this world is not enough?
Like no matter how you try, you're just worthless in their eye?
You've been sticking around, you've been that existence that's not been found.
Like you're invisible in a sense, as you continue to be present.
Ever stop and think about it? about all the ones you overlooked?

Ever stopped and wondered why some people always stood by your side?
Ever took a breath of air, sat back, and wondered if they even care?
If the one you're thinking of even notices you give a fuck?
Ever sat up late at night, whiskey bottle by your side?
As you stare out at the sky and can't help but wonder why.

Why you give so many fucks, why you maintain your interest.
Why your memory won't let go and why you worry at every move.
Worry that you won't be available.
Concerned with the great unknown.
That you put off all your plans, hoping for the fucking chance.
That maybe they would see, but that would be way too easy.

So, you waste another day as you rot quietly, in pain.
Put aside all your goals and you listen to their remorse.
You talk and talk some more.
Then they call you their "gay best friend, brother, sister or cousin" and it strikes a
fucking chord.
Act like it's just a fucking joke but it cuts deeper than they know.

God forbid you have feelings, because you were too busy being
Everything they ever asked, everything they wished they had.
But life is such a drag and you just bottle it away.
As you listen to the rants, as you try and be a friend.
To assist in healing, but they don't acknowledge your efforts.

Then finally you snap, you say fuck you and fuck this!
You walk without remorse.
Throwing all of it to the floor.
When you finally realise, you're chopped liver in their eyes.
If it's karma that's being paid, you pray to die again.
The things done behind the doors.
They made a sociopath for sure, nothing left in the heart.
Your last chance just fell apart.

Ever loved someone so much you don't get in the way, let feelings pile up?
Ever care about the what is, the what ifs and it keeps you up?
To be supportive and sacrifice, everything deep inside.
To lend a listening ear when the voices rage inside?
All those long nights, all the compliments.

Laughed in your stupid face, like you don't mean a god damn thing.
And they wonder why, after a few long years go by.
Just where the fuck you went, because you ghosted them.
In their world, at random but in your mind, a long time coming.
Maybe pay attention and pass your life lesson.
Don't get trapped in your loop and ignore the different views.
The guidance that you have, the voice that gives you plans.
Don't be afraid, chase your dreams today!

Impulse, Envy, Decay

Plays with fire and cries when it burns.
The theory of the apology is accepted after trust is broke.
The forgiveness asked will be revoked.

Palace of glass, you can't let it go.
The thought of the past actions is the final stone.
The decision made, finalizing the shards of what you once called home.

Throw it away, throw with full force.
The walls will collapse as spirits are broke.
Mistakes will be made but sorries have no hold.
Forgiveness is a gift, not a right that you own.

The thoughts of past are drowning us out.
The burning you feel by actions not yours.
Irritation boils until you spiral out of control.
Malevolence feels like justice, until you're left old and alone.

Throwing lit matches in the powder keg room.
Playing with fire, but you already knew.
Deep down inside, where you imprisoned your soul.
Knowing the whole time, you will create a full-fledged asshole.

We get it, everyone already knows.
Your innocent in your endeavor.
The center of the world, you own.
Why consider all the pain you evoke.
Who even cares about the ones no one knows?

Palace of glass is just another broken home.
The people inside suffer alone.
But no one will care; blind eyes, as people move on.
Destroy all connections, collapse all the hope.

Play with fire and burn bridges of gold.
Maybe you're convinced that you had it figured out.
Reach for equality and dissolve all hope.
Perhaps you didn't knot the noose, but you supplied the length of rope.

Years pass by but you will never get another hello.
Nothing will repair what didn't have to be broke.
So, when you break the glass, when you cast your stone.
Acknowledge the voice, the words from your soul.
Make sure you are ready to end all that you know.
Permission isn't needed, but forgiveness isn't owed.
Sorry means nothing when you turn friend to foe.

What They Don't Tell You

Worthless, forgotten, useless, a burden.
A being betrayed, a suicide waiting to happen.
Hopeless, loveless, worthless, abandoned.
How many times trying to speak, but nobody listens.
Silent, angry, hurting, depression.
Twenty years, drowning in a flawed system.
Anguish, torment, lost, unforgiven.
The daily struggle, they called it a blessing.

How many times, how many lives?
How many circles, repeat offenses?
How many people, brothers and sisters?
How many pills, refilled prescriptions?
How many fell into the system?
How many lives, minds left in ruins?
How many lies, recycled lines from the healthy perspective?
How many friends, just a stone made for stepping?
How many tries, breathes should be taken?
How many years before it is accepted?
How much blood? Only takes 3-4 litres.

The cries and the wishes, the fears are so selfish.
The pleads and the bargains.
The guilt placed by those so-called loved ones.
The years of tears and the scars from contemplation.
The whispers turned yelling, the desire, overwhelming.
The friends and the family, the randoms and doctors.
The offered opinion, loss of ambition.
The closing of the throat, tearless corruption.

The compilations, words strung into sentence.
The vultures, the humans.
The agendas they're pushing.

Darkness, restless, causeless, intuition.
The possession of a gift that is not worth giving.
Nagging anxiety, timeless superstition.
They called it wisdom because curse was taken.
Razors, ropes, guns, poison.
Murder weapons used in selfish situation.
Cowardice, weak, conceited decisions.
Show a path that offers more silence.
Tears, stories, remorse, grieving.
The funeral parlour is filled with faking.
Archive, songs, poems, insight.
Left behind, re read and embrace the hindsight.

The voice of a disease that has ruined so many lives.
The desire to help, to explain emotional states.
The logic and insight, the degree of some pain.
To recognize that beating it is actually a lie.
To tell everyone that the battle will rob your life.
The fakeness in a smile that can shine so bright.
The lies in the lines, proclamations of being alright.
They will never understand the hollow deep inside.
To try and explain is the biggest waste of time.
They will tell you it's your fault, you create your own life.
They don't have a clue, just agree and bottle it back inside.
I'm not a doctor but I have something else.
I have real time experience, so I write it out.

Tears, drugs, lies, trust.
Suffer all alone because they all give up.
Therapy, shrinks, hospitals, scrubs.
Sedated because of one thing you said.
Stitches, sickness, visits, corrupt.
Once in the system, they will never forget.
Questions, prying, privacy, distrust.

Your file is now a scapegoat for the rest of your life.
Friends, family, bosses, lovers.
One slip of the tongue and they all jump at your throat.

It's forbidden to speak the truth of what you think.
Label's been placed, there's no escape.
Pry and try to get you to talk.
Don't let your guard down because they will mess you up.
Did you take your pills? Are you sure?
Acting like they know what's up.
Having a bad day no longer exists.
No one is qualified to hear what is leaving your lips.
Friends fade out as you bottle up.
Family feels like work to please their emotions and to ease their hurting hearts.
What is left, where is the support?
Who is gonna step up? Who is gonna want your heart?

Circles, cycles, offenses, repeat.
Tears have long dried and nothing feels complete.
Curious, thinking, sleeping, retreat.
Stay up all night, wishing for sleep.
Mania, panic, anxiety, disease.
There is no cure for feeling make believe.
Jail, rehab, broken, addiction.
No one to talk to, but the drugs never judge you.
Call, message, mail, scream.
I wish all that suffer can find a friend like me.

Blood Without Beauty: Chapter 1

There is a hell.
Inside it I am living.
There was a hope, a chance of redemption.
But how was I to know what door I should have opened?

The voices in my head.
They influenced all the bad decisions.
All the times I bled myself, just chasing a new feeling.

There is a hell and it's the land of the living.
All I have done in life is help my fellow human.
All I know is the unfair hand I was given.
I called out to you, but I guess no one listened.

So alone again.
Inside the white room, I am imprisoned.
Tired more each day, without a corner for me to sit in.
Submerged under the stars, reciting constellations.

The voices in my head.
They influenced all the bad decisions.
All the times I bled myself, just chasing a new feeling.

I called out to you.
But for me, no time was given.
All alone again, I don't know what I am doing.
I just want a friend but I'm the puzzle piece that's always missing.

Everything I am aside from the eternal haunting.
Is everything in which all of you are looking.

Kind and polite, honest and loving.
It's just caged deep, under layers of my wicked.

The voices in my head.
They influenced all the bad decisions.
All the times I bled myself, just chasing a new feeling.

I haven't spoken a word in what feels like forever.
I can't sleep at night, always wake up because of these damned visions.
So, I sit in the dark, take another drink from the bottle.
It tends to subdue the need for bleeding.

This is hell for me, ulcers caused from all the pictures.
My flesh remains but a personal canvas.
I try and fight it.
Try for a silver lining.

The voices in my head.
They influenced all the bad decisions.
All the times I bled myself, just chasing a new feeling.

All I know today, is the echo keeps repeating.
There is a hell.
Inside it, I am living.
There was a hope, a chance of redemption.
But how was I to know what door I should have opened?

How many times will I call upon my reaper?
Cry and beg, take me to a new beginning.
Grant me love, a better tomorrow.
A gentle mental picture.
Take it away!
Tear me out of myself, I can't take another moment.

I beg, as I remain bleeding in the bathroom.
Like the time before, only I'm alone.
Not a patient in the medical system.
No sedatives distributed by the nurses running.
Not gonna wake up, naked in a new room.
To look out the window four inches thick with no recollection.

I wake up, but I'm barely breathing.
Blood clotted, just in time to keep me living.
Bottle still by my side, the light begins to fade in.

Another day in hell, another day of struggling.
Guess I'll get dressed and then the voices kick in.
All I know today, is the echo repeating.
There is a hell.
Inside it I am living
There was a hope, a chance of redemption.
But how was I to know what door I should have opened?

Blood Without Beauty: Chapter 2

Dark hearts can't grab the light.
Through hazel eyes, all flashes in black and white.
Love will come but will it last a night?
Or will it stay and bask in eclipse of a heart and mind alike.

Our hearts were timed just right.
Shadow lurking, but ready for flight.
Our hearts were dark and bright.
Balance of insipid and sweet sacrifice.

Grow tired of the games in life.
Reading between thin lines, the strife.
Grow tired of the sleepless nights.
Only cure was a bottle to put mind to rest.

Off in the distance, you made a move.
If I wasn't so blind, I'd have seen you too.
Hidden in the shadow as the raven called my name.
Heard the sweet whisper but it was too little, too late.

As I took notice, you turned to walk away.
Reciprocating actions as I set sky to flame.
I chased you down and asked you this.
What was it about the shadow I hid, that you saw a place where you could fit?

What is it about my ways, my rants of life and the sisters of fate?
Hard to grasp an idea so vague.
I found your answer, lost in your gaze.

Our hearts were timed just right.
Shadow lurking but ready for flight.
Our hearts were dark and bright.
Balance of insipid and sweet sacrifice.

Pulled from the disaster that was my wake.
I found a partner who shared my pain.
Away with the blood full nights.
Halting all the bittersweet, self sacrifice.
Safe haven joined in the mind.
Both having issues but we don't mind.

This can stand the test of time.
Confide in us before we lose our minds.
This can stand the test of time.
A dark symphony, as bleeding hearts combine.
This can stand the test of time.
Escaping death as we embrace the night.

Our hearts were timed just right.
Shadow lurking, but ready for flight.
Our hearts were dark and bright.
Balance of insipid and sweet sacrifice.

The Siren (You Know)

Look into the eyes of another.
Flashes of words, fragments of sentences.
All that crazy, bottled deep inside.
The conversation had without permission.
I'd say it out loud but I'm too exhausted to make believe.
I'm at the point of: I just don't give a fuck.
Avoiding the what ifs and maybes...

You have questions but you're leery to ask.
You need answers but your still caught up on the past.
You have anger, a resentment, a disappointment, but still no words to explain.
I'm here, I hear; I smile and acknowledge the drain.
Just can't help but feel that vengeance is the end game.
But I don't understand, I just feel insane.
I feel a shame, a sense of villain like you feel betrayed.
Now I find in myself, I pin some blame.

Gaze into the eyes of another, yet again.
Moments of passion, then the prison sentence sets in.
Trapped in a loop, still trying to dissect it.
The shit that plays over in that place; buried, neglected.
Testing the waters, trying to be noticed.
In subtle ways it's like a code your trying to get me to notice.
I'm silent, play stupid as I observe and wait.

So, I sit back; I exist in my own way.
I listen, I dissect and get lost within my analytical ways.
I laugh and you still don't know why, you stare back with uncertainty.
It's like I'm here but lost within the haze.

As I stare into those eyes, I fade out, into the vortex in my mind; it always feels like days.
I drift off to the border of time and space.
As I replay all the seconds from all those days.
I rake, I comb, and I sort.
I pick it apart just to pick at it some more.
Lost, dazed and confused.
Maybe you can relate? Maybe you feel the same as I do?

Strangers that met in such awkward timing.
Subtle introduction as you pin me with treason.
You tore me apart before I said hello.
I read it in your eyes as I picked at your soul.
Victim of circumstance and the need to escape.
The need to talk, to feel like someone can relate.
The need for a friend, for someone to listen as you deal with your rage.
Inconvenience had become my place.
So, I left before shit blew up in my face.

Funny how we just know it's time to leave.
How a person can feel a certain way.
To feel the push that enables us to see.
That moment when you just know.
It will be different the next time we meet.
Until that is all hindsight and you're lost in a daze.
Just looking back as you remember certain things.
Too many questions with too many fates.
Too many problems that I'll never see.
Too many times I get stuck in this space.
Then I snap back, you're staring.
All I got is "what did you say?".

Too many times I wanted to say.
Too many words rattle my brain.
You would be surprised on how stubborn I'll be.
You would be surprised at just what it is, I think.
All of these problems are for a reason.
All of this nonsense is a necessary evil.
To the time, I patiently waited.

To this day, still, procrastination.
You would be shook at the struggle I feel.
You still have my support because you stayed real.
All this bullshit caused from lack of words.
All this speculation but the ball's in your court.
Too many nights with minimal sleep.
Too many times, thinking too deep.